*Kevin Riggs*

K E V I N  R I G G S

# Failing *Like* Jesus

Redefining Your
Perception of Success

7219
randall house
114 Bush Rd. | Nashville, TN 37217 | randallhouse.com

© 2010 by Kevin Riggs

Published by Randall House
114 Bush Road
Nashville, TN 37217

www.randallhouse.com

Printed in the United States of America

13-ISBN 9780892656028

I consider myself extremely blessed to have married my high-school sweetheart, Misty; and so it is to her that I dedicate this book. She has stood by me, and walked with me through whatever success I have had. I love you.

# Table of Contents

Introduction . . . . . . . . . . . . . . . . . . . . . . . . . . . . . . . . . . . . . . . . ix

Chapter 1    Misunderstanding Jesus . . . . . . . . . . . . . . . . . . . . . . 1

Chapter 2    Skeletons in the Closet. . . . . . . . . . . . . . . . . . . . . 13

Chapter 3    The Time Is Now, but Not Yet . . . . . . . . . . . . . . . 25

Chapter 4    You Can't Go Home Again . . . . . . . . . . . . . . . . . 37

Chapter 5    The "B" Team . . . . . . . . . . . . . . . . . . . . . . . . . . . . 51

Chapter 6    Some Say He Was an Outlaw. . . . . . . . . . . . . . . . . 65

Chapter 7    Was Jesus a Republican or Democrat? . . . . . . . . . . . 79

Chapter 8    A Reputation for Discarding His Reputation. . . . . . . 93

Chapter 9    A Terrible Temper . . . . . . . . . . . . . . . . . . . . . . . . 105

Chapter 10   This Is Not What I Signed Up For. . . . . . . . . . . . . 113

Chapter 11   The Darkest Day in History . . . . . . . . . . . . . . . . . . 125

Chapter 12   That's the End of That . . . . . . . . . . . . . . . . . . . . . . 135

Chapter 13   Now It's Your Turn. . . . . . . . . . . . . . . . . . . . . . . . 147

# Introduction

Before I began my first pastorate I took a respected pastor friend to lunch for advice.

"If I were your son," I asked him, "and there was only one thing you could tell me about ministry, what would it be?"

My friend had been a pastor for many years, so without hesitation he answered, "Always remember that your walk with Christ is more important than your work for Christ."

This wise mentor went on to explain that if I based my self-esteem on how my ministry was going I would eventually be an emotional wreck. But if I based my identity on whom I am in Christ, I could remain calm and steady during the storms of life. I understood the wisdom of his advice intellectually, but a few years later I would comprehend the wisdom of his advice experientially, coming to embrace it intimately.

> *Always remember that your walk with Christ is more important than your work for Christ.*

## I'm Not Having Any Kind of "Wonderful" Anymore

The very first law in the *4 Spiritual Laws* states, "God loves you, and offers a wonderful plan for your life."[1] I remember thinking the first time I heard that promise: *Sounds great! Who doesn't want to experience God's wonderful plan for their lives?* But after following the black and white printed steps to salvation in the booklet, then looking at my circumstances in the weeks, months, and years following, it was easy to conclude: *If this is God's wonderful plan for my life, He must not love me very much.*

Perhaps you, like me, have looked heavenward and asked, "Hey Lord! How about a plan B for me because I'm not having any kind of 'wonderful' anymore?"

If you are remotely perceptive, you realize that some of life's circumstances are a direct result of decisions you've made, while many other situations occur because of other people's actions. Of course, there are other circumstances beyond the control of anyone. For example, you didn't choose to be born to parents with a matching set of emotional baggage or a heart condition that could shorten your life. You had no choice over your natural abilities or the color of your skin. It wasn't your decision to be born in the city, state, or county in which you were born.

When I was in seventh grade I ruptured my spleen playing football and almost died. I had dreams of playing in the NFL. That injury shattered that dream. How is that part of a wonderful plan? When I was eighteen I purchased my first vehicle—a beautiful, mist orange, 1984, Nissan pick-up. Six days later I rear-ended someone's car. Guess whose fault it was? Guess who got a ticket? My parents, the other driver, my girlfriend who was in the passenger's seat, the insurance company . . . none thought this was the wonderful plan God had for their lives.

I spent 13 years at the first church I pastored. Those years were fundamental to my development as a minister. Two years after I resigned, because of reasons I don't understand and can't explain, that same church was a shell of what it was when I left. They were in danger of closing their doors for good. How is that failure consistent with God's wonderful plan?

One professional athlete wins a championship ring his rookie year, while a veteran plays twenty years and never gets the same opportunity. What's up with that? Why does it seem God's plan is more wonderful for some than for others?

I don't know the answers, but I do know that first spiritual law is true! God does have a wonderful plan for my life, and somehow that plan includes ups and downs, peaks and valleys. What I need to do is trust God's plan for my life and believe His plan is better for my life than my plan. Yet, often, I am confused about God's plan.

My gut tells me the reason for my confusion is because my definition of wonderful, and God's definition, is not the same. What's more, I am willing to bet God's idea of success is different from my idea . . . or your idea. Success, for many, is measured by outward, tangible things. Success is measured by how are peers view us—accolades and applause—or by the amount of influence we have in our sphere of influence. We value success and hard work and commitment. And while all those things are important, somehow I think God measures success differently. Sometimes, what people perceive as failures, God perceives as success and sometimes what we think is successful, God judges as failures.

What's my conclusion? *God's plan for success includes moments of perceived failure.* The road we all must travel includes paths of difficulties and detours of pain. Jesus is our primary example of this truth.

Jesus appeared to have failed miserably on many occasions. Yet in the end, He was the living, dying epitome of success. Jesus "failed" His way all the way to the cross. Somehow, I admit I don't understand, being like Jesus means that at times I will be perceived as a failure.

The process of becoming like Jesus involves going through and sharing "like" experiences as He. Jesus said, "If the world hates you, keep in mind that it hated me first . . . . If they persecuted me, they will persecute you also. If they obeyed my teaching, they will obey yours also." (John 15:18, 20) A disciple of Jesus will experience the same things Jesus experienced; and the things that you and I experience, Jesus has already experienced. Paul wrote, "I want to know Christ and the power of his resurrection and the fellowship of sharing in his sufferings, becoming like him in his death, and so, somehow, to attain to the resurrection from the dead" (Philippians 3:10-11).

So, are you ready to climb and stumble and fall and climb again—all the way to the top? Are you ready for God to put all the pieces together? Are you ready to be like Jesus? The bad news is bad things happen; it's an

> *A disciple of Jesus will experience the same things Jesus experienced; and the things that you and I experience, Jesus has already experienced.*

unavoidable part of any real journey to ultimate success. The good news is *you are not alone.* Even the Messiah, the Son of God, knows how you feel. The writer of Hebrews put it this way, "For we do not have a high priest who is unable to sympathize with our weaknesses, but we have one who has been tempted in every way, just as we are—yet was without sin. Let us then approach the throne of grace with confidence, so that we may receive mercy and find grace to help us in our time of need" (Hebrews 4:15-16).

**ENDNOTE**

[1] From *Have You Heard of the Four Spiritual Laws?* Written by Bill Bright © Copyright 1965-2008 Campus Crusade for Christ® and Bright Media Foundation. All rights reserved. Used by permission.

# 1  Misunderstanding Jesus

## Imagine for a moment . . .

From His childhood home in Nazareth, Jesus could see the snow-capped peaks of Mount Hermon in the distance. As a child, He spent hours gazing at the mountain and dreaming of one day climbing to the top.

Jesus remembered that childhood dream as He and His disciples started their journey up that mountain. At 1,150 feet above sea level, on the base of Mount Hermon, Caesarea Philippi was the perfect place to rest and reflect, if even for a moment. At the base of the mountain a deep cavern full of water, similar to the ones found in Greece, served as a source for the Jordan River. On this spot the Greeks built a shrine to their god Pan, whom they believed dwelt in grottos and wandered on the mountains.[1]

It had been days since Jesus had stopped to rest. Life had been a blur of preaching, teaching, and healing the sick. In a rare quiet moment, walking with His friends, Jesus asked an interesting question. "Who do people say I am? (Mark 8:27).[2] Jesus wanted to know what other people thought of Him.

> *People rejected Jesus, not because they didn't like Him, but because they misunderstood who He was and what He was about.*

## Jesus Tried to Be Understood

From the beginning of His ministry, Jesus was clear about who He was and why He was here. His mission was basically simple: He announced that the Kingdom of God was near. He came to serve, not to be served. He healed the sick, forgave sins, taught with authority, and performed miracles. Still, the masses just didn't get that He was the Messiah—God in the flesh, God in human form. They thought He was a prophet, a teacher, a good person, someone to follow, someone full of wisdom, etc. Their answers generally showed respect, but most often a lack of understanding.

With the possible exception of the religious leaders, people rejected Jesus, not because they didn't like Him, but because they misunderstood who He was and what He was about.

While His question to the disciples shows He was concerned if people where understanding who He was and what He was about, Jesus lived, not to please others, but to please God. How do we know this is true? Jesus said, "My food . . . is to do the will of him who sent me and to finish his work" (John 4:34). Pleasing His heavenly Father was as necessary and nourishing to Him as lunch or dinner, bread or water.

> *When we get our minds off of God's approval and focus on our ministries . . . life becomes complicated.*

Carrying out His Father's instructions was His total focus. This focus kept Him from being sidetracked by the unimportance of the immediate or the approval of others. Jesus served and obeyed an audience of One; but He loved, cared for, and ultimately died for, a world of billions.

As a pastor who observes and talks with many other pastors I've discovered an interesting thing: *When we get our minds off of God's approval and focus on our ministries (or whether or not we impress others), life becomes complicated.* This is not only true of ministers, but it is also true of everyone who follows Jesus.

I have a friend who pastors a mega-church.[3] I have spent my career pastoring small and medium sized churches.[4] One day while eating lunch with this pastor friend, listening to some of his struggles, it dawned on me—*he has the same fears I have. If he quits looking for God's approval, he will get sidetracked as quickly as I will!*

Mega-church pastors feel constant pressure to impress others. People tend to see them as "experts," asking them to speak at conferences and lead seminars to explain how others can grow their mini-ministries into super-sized sanctuaries, overflowing with saints. Ironically, many pastors of huge congregations secretly fear that one day the applause will cease and they will be discovered as flawed human beings, not super-spiritual giants. Some are afraid their parishioners will eventually realize they are not as good as they appear and the ministries they have built are just a house of cards, waiting to crumble.

On the other hand, often times, small church pastors don't feel like frauds; they feel like failures. No one wants their opinions; no one wants to hear what they have to say. They feel left out, unappreciated, and are afraid people will not respect them because of their small, "insignificant" ministries. Almost weekly, the temptation a small church pastor faces is to look over his sparse congregation and be reminded of his own inadequacies.

Whether it's feelings of being a fraud or a failure, all leaders, indeed, most Christians, have fears and a natural desire to seek approval from others. Though it is a human inclination, yielding to these fears makes life complicated and ministry unfulfilling. I can get emotionally derailed for days over someone's false impression of me—putting all sorts of energy into setting the record straight. Interestingly, Jesus took these things in stride. He continued with the work at hand without hesitation because

> *Life is simplified when you decide to live for an audience of One. Until you accept who you are in God's eyes, you will either focus on applause or failure and miss the whole point.*

He knew who He was. What others thought of Him did not shape His understanding of Himself. Most of us can't imagine a self-esteem so healthy and centered in God where very little thought was given to others' opinions.

Life is simplified when you decide to live for an audience of One. Until you accept who you are in God's eyes, you will either focus on applause or failure and miss the whole point.

## Misplaced Identity

In August of 1989, as a 23 year-old, full of unwavering commitment and unfaltering optimism, Steve stepped into his role as pastor of a small, dying church. His moment had arrived. It was time for him to shine, take on the world, and fulfill God's plan for his life. Steve figured, at the most, it would take four or five years to grow his church from 30 to at least 1,000. After all, he came to the congregation armed with youthful enthusiasm, a purpose-filled plan, a seminary degree, and a unanimous vote from the congregation.

Much to Steve's astonishment, his church did not grow as quickly as he thought it would. After four years he struggled to get 80 people in the pews for Sunday worship. Steve dreaded the all-important question from his denominational peers: "So how many are you runnin' in Sunday School?" Progress had been painfully slow, but it had been steady— at least that's what he kept telling himself. Deep down, however, Steve felt like a complete failure. His identity was wrapped up in his *work* for Christ, not his *walk* with Him. Steve wrote in his journal:

Tuesday, October 5 (6:15 a.m.) – *Lord, I don't understand what is happening . . . . The church is not growing like it should and I have just come through a conflict with a church leader. Furthermore, I feel an undercurrent of griping and complaining among the members. Why are things so difficult for me? Why do other churches seem to grow without any effort and all I do is laborious? I am grateful for what has been accomplished, but when are You going to send miraculous growth my way? What am I doing wrong? What do I need to confess and change? Lord, I am giving my all to You, and all I am getting in return is heartache and depression. Please forgive me, but I don't know where else to turn. No one understands like You and I know no one loves me like You. All I know is I can't continue like this. Help me, please.*

In short, Steve was living for the applause of others instead of the applause of One. He knew if he did not change, he would soon be a ministerial wash-out, a shipwrecked statistic, all before he reached 30 years of age. Steve needed to narrow his focus to one goal, to pleasing the one and only God.

But what does living for an audience of One mean in practical day-to-day life?

For starters, it means being willing to let go of your dream, exchanging it for God's dream. When we give up our dreams it can feel as though we are admitting defeat. It sounds painful to give up your dreams of success (however you define that success), but, in the long run, it is much easier than clinging to a corpse of a man-made plan. God's dream for me is to be like Jesus. That is His dream for you as well; and though it may not seem so at this moment, it is a far greater privilege and joy than anything you can ever dream for yourself. The apostle Paul wrote, "Now to him who is able to do immeasurably more than all we ask or imagine, according to his power that is at work within us, to him be glory in the church and in Christ Jesus throughout all generations, for ever and ever! Amen" (Ephesians 3:20-21).

Second, living for an audience of One means letting go of other people's dreams for you, real or perceived. We all have our personal "everybodys." That little, mental panel of people who sit on your shoulder when you are making choices for your life—which brand of shaving cream to buy or what career you should follow. Usually our "Everybody" is made up of three or four people whose opinions have come to mean much to us, which isn't a bad thing unless they mean more than God's opinion of you.

> *Steve knew if he did not change, he would soon be a ministerial wash-out, a shipwrecked statistic, all before he reached 30 years of age.*

Here are a two examples of what I mean:

A young lady decides to go to medical school, even though her dream (and God's will) is to be a high school algebra teacher. Yet because her father and grandfather are doctors, it is what's expected. A young man goes into business so he can take over the family store, but deep down he knows God has called him to be a missionary. He goes on to have a successful career but in rare, contemplative moments, his heart whispers, *you are not living God's dream for you.*

Why do so many people live someone else's dream for them instead of God's dream for them? I suppose many people think it's easier to disappoint a God you can't see than family and friends you see everyday. Still, I wonder how many people are living someone else's vision? How many young men and women followed someone else's dream only to wake up to a nightmare, struggling to live an authentic life? What would have happened if Jesus would have lived His life based on what others thought of Him?

As I thought about these things, I realized Jesus would have been perceived as a failure by most people's standards. Sure, there were a few high points, but instead of being famous, He was infamous. Instead of being liked, He was crucified. Most people did not come to Him to learn about the kingdom of God; they came to see a show and to get something—a healing, a meal, or a thrill. Jesus wasn't at all impressed or enamored by celebrity status or earthly success. In fact, He was often eager to slip away anonymously from the crowds that could have fed His ego with praise and applause. Jesus was just as satisfied with a group of 12 as He was a crowd of 12,000.

God's dream for you is beyond your wildest fantasy, which may be the reason it is so hard to follow His lead. Sometimes what God wants for us just seems too big, too much for our minds to handle, too good to be true.

What God wants from us more than anything else is a relationship. He wants us to trust Him, to follow Him, and to obey Him. He wants us to live for an audience of One. When we live for Him, He guides us into a bigger plan for our lives. He gives us what we need to handle God-sized dreams, and His God-sized dream is for us to follow Jesus so He can remake us into Jesus' image.

Are you living someone else's dream? Are you pursuing someone else's life? Are you ready to give up that dream for God's? Don't worry, you are not being asked to hand your life over to Someone you can't know well or trust. You can know God, and He desperately wants to know you; and God has proven Himself trustworthy time and time again.

## Jesus Is My Spouse

Agnes Gonxha Bojaxhiu was born to an upper-middle class family.[5] By the age of 12, she felt called by God to aid the poor and downcast. At eighteen years of age, inspired by Jesuit missionaries working in Bengal, India, Agnes left home to work with a community of Irish nuns in a mission in Calcutta, India. She changed her name to Sister Teresa, and later became known as Mother Teresa.

One day, in front of a Calcutta hospital, Mother Teresa found a woman half eaten by maggots and rats. She sat with the woman until she died; and then set out on a campaign to build a shelter where people could die with dignity. Her shelter, the Nimal Hriday[6] Home for Dying Destitutes, became a place were the uncared for and unacceptable were washed, fed, and allowed to die in a place filled with love.

In 1979, Mother Teresa won the Noble Peace Prize. Accepting the

> **The Looking Glass Self**
> Sociologist describe the process of seeing ourselves the way we perceive others see us as the "looking glass self." The idea is that other people represent a mirror in which we see ourselves. As a result, we become what we think others want us to become.

award and wearing the same one-dollar, white sari she had worn for years, she said, "I choose the poverty of our poor people. But I am grateful to receive (the Nobel) in the name of the hungry, the naked, the homeless, of the crippled, of the blind, of the lepers, of all those people who feel unwanted, unloved, uncared-for throughout society, people that have become a burden to the society and are shunned by everyone."[7] She used the $192,000 prize money to help finance her charitable work.

When Mother Teresa opened her home in Calcutta, local people complained and tried to get the police commissioner to evict her. Moved by the misery he saw, the commissioner said he would evict her only if the local people decided to take over her work. No one took the commissioner's offer.

During her life of ministry Mother Teresa was accused of impropriety because she accepted contributions without questioning the source. She was criticized for exploiting her fame, and of being a spiritual colonialists. Throughout her life, people questioned her motives, rejected her attempts to love, twisted her words, and misunderstood her reasons for doing what she did. Based on what others, at the time, thought of her, it would be easy to conclude that Mother

Teresa was a failure.

However, Mother Teresa knew who she was. She responded to these criticisms by saying, "No matter who says what, you should accept it with a smile and do your own work."[8] Her self-worth was in Jesus. She said, "Jesus is my God. Jesus is my Spouse. Jesus is my Life. Jesus is my only Love. Jesus is my All in All. Jesus is my everything."[9]

Do you have that type of confidence?

Do you know how God *really* feels about you?

Are you overly concerned with what others think?

Jesus asked His friends, "So tell Me, who do people say I am? What do people think of me?" If He were to ask that question today, how would people answer? How would you answer? Larry Norman, one of the early Christian contemporary musicians of the mid-1970s, gave great insight into possible answers in his song, "The Outlaw."

> *Jesus is my God. Jesus is my Spouse. Jesus is my Life. Jesus is my only Love. Jesus is my All in All. Jesus is my Everything.*
> —Mother Teresa

*Some say he was an outlaw,*
*that he roamed across the land*
*With a band of unschooled ruffians*
*and a few old fishermen.*
*No one knew just where he came from*
*or exactly what he'd done,*
*But they said it must be something bad*
*that kept him on the run.*

*Some say he was a poet,*
*that he'd stand upon a hill*
*And his voice could calm an angry crowd,*
*or make the waves stand still.*
*That he spoke in many parables*
*that few could understand,*
*But the people stood for hours*
*just to listen to this man.*

*Some say he was a sorcerer,*
*a man of mystery,*
*He would walk upon the water,*
*he could make the blind man see,*
*That he conjured wine at weddings*
*and did tricks with fish and bread,*
*That he talked of being born again*
*and raised people from the dead.*

*Some say a politician who spoke of being free.*
*He was followed by the masses on the shores of Galilee.*
*He spoke out against corruption*
*and he bowed to no decree,*
*And they feared his strength*
*and power so they nailed him to a tree.*

*Some say he was the Son of God, a man above all men.*
*But, he came to be a servant and to set us free from sin.*
*And that's who I believe he was 'cause that's what I believe,*
*And I think we should get ready, 'cause it's time for us to leave.*[10]

An outlaw? A poet? A sorcerer? A politician? The Son of God? Who was Jesus? Who is Jesus? God said, "This is my Son, whom I love; with him I am well pleased" (Matthew 3:17).

Who are you? God says, "This is my son or my daughter, whom I love; with him and with her I am well pleased." Though you may doubt it at times, the God of the universe says, "For I know the plans I have for you . . . plans to prosper you and not to harm you, plans to give you hope and a future" (Jeremiah 29:11). The God who created you made you for a purpose. He knows what makes you tick. He knows what will give your life meaning. He knows how to give you peace and fulfillment. Not only does He know these things, He desperately wants to give them to you. As God's dear child, you can be sure His dreams are even bigger and better than yours. God loves you and knows you better than you love and know yourself. His opinion of you is the only one that truly matters. If you really believe this, it will give you the fortitude to follow Him, and Him alone, even if it means you will be misunderstood; even it if means others perceive you as a failure.

Like you, Jesus was misunderstood (sometimes by his closest friends and followers), but because He knew who He really was in His Father's eyes, He walked onward and upward, one foot in front of the other, towards a cross . . . and a tomb . . . and a glorious resurrection that would free His children from Satan's grasp. He fulfilled His mission and focused on the audience of One and even when the world labeled Him "failure" and ridiculed His ways, Jesus tuned His ear toward heaven and heard the applause of His Father.

That was all He needed.

Indeed, all that truly mattered.

Is it all that matters to you?

# ENDNOTES

[1]The god Pan was feared by those who had to travel the woods at night. Our word *panic*, comes from the mythological figure Pan, and was originally used to describe sudden fright without any visible cause.

[2]The direct quote is from Mark 8:27, however, Matthew 16:13 and Luke 9:18, tell the same story, with a little different wording.

[3]A mega-church is defined as a church with more than 2,000 people in attendance each week.

[4]I have pastored churches that range in attendance from 25 to 500.

[5]Agnes Gonxha Bojaxhiu was born August 26, 1910.

[6]Nimal Hriday means "Pure Heart."

[7]"Mother Teresa: A Profile." 1997. The Associated Press. www.cnn.com/WORLD/9709/mother.teresa.

[8]"Mother Teresa, patron of the poor, dead at 87." http://www.lubbock-online.com/news/090697/mother_teresa.htm. Copyright Lubbock Avalanche—Journal 1997.

[9]http://www.ewtn.com/motherteresa/words.htm.

[10]"The Outlaw" by Larry Norman from the album "Only Visiting This Planet", 1972.

# Questions for Discussion

1. What do people say about Jesus today? How would you answer Jesus' question in Matthew 16:13?

2. How should you look at yourself in relationship to your heavenly Father?

3. What do you think it means to "live for an audience of One?" How would doing so change your life?

4. Which is easier, letting go of your dreams for yourself or letting go of other people's dreams for you? Why? Recall in your life where you were living someone else's dream for you, instead of your own dream for yourself, or God's dream for you?

5. In what ways might you be misunderstood if you decide to "live for an audience of One?" Give an example where you were misunderstood for striving to be like Jesus? What happened? How did you respond?

# 2 Skeletons in the Closet

A quick glance at Jesus' family tree seems impressive. His roots go all the way back to Abraham through King David.[1] However, upon closer inspection, you find skeletons in His closet. Three out of the four women mentioned in His lineage were not even Jewish. Tamar[2] pretended to be a prostitute. Rahab[3] actually was a prostitute. Bathsheba[4] was the object of the most famous scandal in the Old Testament. It was because of His questionable ancestry that many Jews rejected Him.

Not only was His family tree questionable, Jesus was born into a hostile environment. Alexander the Great—hundreds of years before Jesus was born—tried to bring the whole world under one language, one culture, and one way of thinking. By the time of Jesus' birth, people everywhere dressed like the Greeks, built like the Greeks, played like the Greeks, and spoke like the Greeks. The only exception was in Palestine . . . Jesus' homeland.[5]

From the time of Alexander the Great until just before the birth of Jesus, tens of thousands of Palestinians were killed during skirmishes with the Roman Army. Things settled down during the time of Herod the Great, but Palestine was still an explosive, inflammable place to live. The whole area had a reputation as a breeding ground for revolutionaries. The most hostile of the three provinces in Palestine was Galilee. Like today's Middle East, Palestine was a hotbed of revolts and threats of revolts.

People from Galilee were de-

> In his wonderful book, *The Jesus I Never Knew*, Philip Yancey comments, "These shady ancestors show that Jesus entered human history in the raw, a willing descendant of its shame. In contrast, Herod the Great, reigning king at Jesus' birth, had his genealogical records destroyed out of vanity because He wanted no one to compare his background with others."

spised by their Jewish brothers and sisters. After the conquest by Tiglath-Pilesser, king of Assyria, in 732 B.C., Galilee was repopulated by a colony of heathen immigrants, intermarrying with the Jews. By Jesus' day, most Galileans were of mixed race, and the "pure" Jews in Jerusalem struggled to accept them. On one occasion, teachers of the Law criticized Jesus, saying, "Look into it, and you will find that a prophet does not come out of Galilee" (John 7:52). Galileans had a distinct accent and dialect and were the object of extreme prejudices.[6]

Within Palestine, the province of Galilee was most despised. The worst Galilean town by reputation was Nazareth, Jesus' childhood home. Nazareth was a farming community, a small town on the backside of nowhere. The people from Nazareth were the butt of ethnic jokes from both Jews and Gentiles who lived in the surrounding area. It was a town known for its wickedness and despised by the Jews. Close to Nazareth was a large military headquarters set up by the Romans, bringing with it all the vices of a military town. No wonder Nathanael doubted who Jesus was, saying, "Nazareth! Can anything good come from there?" (John 1:46).

Not only was Jesus born in the wrong town in the wrong part of Galilee, Jesus and His family were poor. When he was eight days old, his family went to the temple, but they were too poor to afford the customary sacrificial lamb. Instead, Mary and Joseph offered a pair of doves and two young pigeons.[7] Adding to their low social standing, Jesus and His family spent His infancy as refugees, fleeing from a king who

---

Sometime between 334-331 B.C., Alexander the Great defeated Persia and took control of the Roman Empire. Alexander permitted the Jews to observe their religion, and even gave them a measure of tax freedom, but he sought to bring them under Greek culture, known as *Hellenism.*

Israel remained under Greek control from the time of Alexander the Great until 63 B.C. Between 63 and 37 B.C., more than 150,000 Palestinians were killed in revolutionary uprisings. In 31 B.C., an earthquake rocked the area, killing 30,000 people. The Jews called such events "pangs of the Messiah," and prayed for God to do something, anything. By the time of Jesus' birth the anticipation that a messiah was coming was at a fever pitch.

wanted Him murdered. The gifts the wise men brought Jesus were used to help the family survive during their exile in Egypt.

Joseph, Jesus' earthly stepfather, worked hard as a carpenter. But he never reached above the "working poor" of the area. More than likely Joseph died before Jesus began His ministry, perhaps even before He was a teenager, which made Jesus the man of the house, placing on him the responsibility of providing for his mother, brother, and sisters.[8]

Are you beginning to get the picture? Instead of being a nice and neat fairytale existence, Jesus was born into a very real world as a very real person, and His living conditions set Him up to be a failure. No one would ever guess, by His background, that He was the Son of God. In His day, many people were looking for the Messiah, but no one would have guessed it would be Jesus of Nazareth.

## Everyone Has Obstacles

Everyone has obstacles to overcome. No one chooses the time, place, and manner of his or her birth; and no one chooses his or her parents. From the very beginning, the odds were against Jesus being Someone who could change the world. To those living during this time, He was conceived out of wedlock to a poor teenage mother who others must have considered delusional, claiming to be a virgin while pregnant. His family had no place to call home until they settled in a small, poverty-stricken village. He would always be Joseph's stepson, never knowing what it was like to have a human, biological dad. And He lived during a time of tremendous upheaval and political turmoil.

If the life of Jesus teaches anything, it teaches that your family's dysfunction, or poverty, or low status, or wealth, or fame does not define the direction your life has to take. God uses unusual, and often times difficult circumstances, to bring about His ultimate plan. Somehow the timing and manner of Jesus' birth, His flight to Egypt and return to Nazareth to grow up in poverty and in a hostile environment, were all part of God's plan. Jesus was no accident, and neither were you.

Trula was born on June 7, 1924, in the shadow of the Smoky Mountains of east Tennessee. Her family was poor before the Great Depression; during the Great Depression they were despondent. When Trula was 3 years old, her mother died of tuberculosis. Unable to care for her, Trula's father gave her to his sister. Her childhood resembled the bad part of Cinderella's story.

As a young teenager, Trula's uncle informed her she would have to quit school to help care for the children and take over more of the housework. Determined to continue her education, Trula gathered her things in secret, and left her aunt and uncle's home. At 15 years of age, Trula moved into an orphanage in Greenville, Tennessee.

Born during the depression, poor and parentless, Trula Cronk seemingly had slim chance to live a good life. But her family background did not determine her future direction. Trula overcame tremendous odds, graduating from high school and then college. In college she met her soul mate, Dan. The two of them answered the call to missions, and served 25 years in India, sharing the gospel, starting churches, and building orphanages.[9]

> *No matter your past or present, you were not an accident; God has a plan for your life.*

It would have been easy for Trula to believe her life was a waste of time. Instead, she chose to believe her life was an adventure. In her autobiography she wrote, "I believe that I was created to be Christian and that the Christian way is written into the very structure of my being . . . . The starting point for experiencing a full and abundant life is in the statement 'God loves me' . . . . It does not mean that He approves of everything I do, or that He admires my character. Nevertheless He loves me. He loves what He has made and He is always waiting for me to turn to Him for help in finishing what He began."[10]

No matter your past or present, God had a reason for creating you. David wrote, "I praise you because I am fearfully and wonderfully made; your works are wonderful, I know that full well. My frame was not hidden from you when I was made in the secret place. When I was woven together in the depths of the earth, your eyes saw my unformed body. All the days ordained for me were written in your book before one of them came to be" (Psalm 139:14-16).

Amazing! God has your life planned from beginning to end. He loves you and wants what is best for you. You may have thought you were a mistake. Your dad may have said you would not amount to anything; your mom may have deserted you; and you may have been labeled a "troublemaker" by teachers at school, but none of that matters. God knows you, and He can turn your dysfunction into His direction for your life. He can also turn your abuse into abundance, and if you were blessed with a happy childhood, He can bring you into an even more glorious adulthood.

God is in control when things are comfortable, but He is also in control when things are chaotic. God knows all, sees all, and is in all. The Bible says, "For by him all things were created: things in heaven and on earth, visible and invisible, whether thrones or powers or rulers or authorities; all things were created by him and for him. He is before all things, and in him all things hold together" (Colossians 1:16-17).

## The Bottom Floor

Have you ever wondered why the top floor of a high-rise building is called the "penthouse"? Have you ever wondered why the penthouse is the most expensive floor? While in college, working as a security guard at a high-rise condominium complex, I learned why.

Everyone who lived in this complex were millionaires. But being a millionaire only carries so much prestige. The high rise, itself, was a measuring stick. The higher up a person lived, the richer he or she was, and the more prestigious the position. Thus, the person on top was the "top dog." Living in the penthouse was a big deal, and the people took this ranking seriously.

One family, who lived in this high rise, had a town home

that took up two floors. Their main entrance was on the sixth floor, but on the seventh floor was a door best described as a "back" door or "side" door. The only thing on the seventh floor was their bedrooms. Their living areas and kitchen were on the sixth floor. (I know this because on several occasions I had to go into their home to make sure things like the stove had been turned off when they were out of town, or let workman in during the day to repair one thing or another.)

Without fail, when this family got on the elevator by themselves, or with people who lived below them, they would get off at the sixth floor. But if they got on the elevator with someone who lived above them, they would exit on the seventh floor. On one occasion I saw the wife get on the elevator with several bags of groceries. I offered to carry the bags up for her but on this occasion she declined. Then, as the elevator door was closing, a person got on who lived above her. With great curiosity I watched the lighted floor numbers above the elevator door to see which floor she would exit. And guess what? Although her kitchen was on the sixth floor, she got off on the seventh floor! I laughed at the thought of her carrying her groceries into her bedroom, just to impress someone else.

I have spent a number of years teaching Sociology at a local community college in Nashville, Tennessee. One of my favorite topics to discuss each semester is "Social Stratification," the system by which society ranks people in a hierarchy. Whether we like it or not, we are taught to evaluate people by certain conditions that society values as good and bad, better or worse. In extreme situations, societies develop a "caste system" where people are born into a category where they must remain their whole lives. In more democratic societies a "class system" develops where people are ranked by both birth and individual achievement. In theory, a "class system" is an "open system," meaning individuals can better themselves and move up the stratification scale. It is also possible, within an open system, to move down the scale as well. But in reality, most people live and die in the class in which they were born. In our society a person's social ranking is determined by things like income, wealth, power, occupation, schooling, ancestry, race, ethnicity, and gender; and where a person ranks can affect his or her health, education, and opportunities. The point is this, in every area of societal ranking, Jesus was on the lowest rung.

Jesus lived on the bottom floor. Yet He rose higher than anyone else in history. Paul wrote, "Your attitude should be the same as that of Christ Jesus: Who, being in very nature God, did not consider equality with God something to be grasped, but made himself nothing, taking the very nature of a servant, being made in human likeness. And being found in appearance as a man, he humbled himself and became obedient to death—even death on a cross! Therefore God exalted him to the highest place and gave him the name that is above every name, that at the name of Jesus every knee should bow, in heaven and on earth and under the earth, and every tongue confess that Jesus Christ is Lord, to the glory of God the Father" (Philippians 2:5-11).

## Amazing the Qualified

What floor are you on? Where does society rank you? Does it seem like the whole world is against you? Have you been told you will never amount to anything because of your past? Have you given up because you don't have the education, background, money, or family to "succeed"?

Don't give up. God wants to use you. From God's perspective, everyone is qualified. God loves to use the ordinary to do the extraordinary. He used an ordinary shrub to convince an ordinary man like Moses to take his ordinary life and ordinary training and deliver His people from slavery in an extraordinary way.

God took an ordinary boy, with an ordinary sling and five ordinary rocks to bring down a not so ordinary giant.

He took an ordinary teenage girl, and chose her to be the extraordinary mother of Jesus.

Then, God turned everything upside down by choosing to take His extraordinary Son and send Him to the most ordinary village to live an ordinary life so He could die a cruel death and redeem us in a most extraordinary way.

Why does God enjoy using the ordinary to do the extraordinary? He enjoys it because He loves to use people who are weak to show His strength. God said, "My power is made perfect in weakness" (2 Corinthians 12:9).

God chooses the most unusual people. Jacob, was the younger brother of Esau, yet, God chose Jacob over Esau.

Joseph was hated by his brothers, sold into slavery, and falsely accused of sexual misconduct, yet he was chosen by God to lead Egypt through a horrible famine.

There was nothing worth noting in any of the original 12 disciples; each one was ordinarily ordinary. Even the great apostle Paul said he was the worst of all sinners.[11]

God loves to use people who are weak to show the world His power so there will be no doubt as to His strength. This is great news because most of us are ordinary. Most of us will live our lives in anonymity. Very few people are known by anyone except their family and friends, and after death all of us are quickly forgotten. But God knows who you are. He knows everything about you, and He wants to use you, in your weakness, to show the world His strength.

## Astounding the Wise

God loves to use the simple things in life to astound the wise. The Bible says, "For the foolishness of God is wiser than man's wisdom .... But God chose the foolish things of the world to shame the wise .... He chose the lowly things of this world and the despised things—and the things that are not—to nullify the things that are" (1 Corinthians 1:25, 27-28).

> *God loves to use people who are weak to show the world His power so there will be no doubts to His strength.*

From society's point of view, Jesus had every reason to fail. But He beat the odds. He overcame all obstacles. He proved everyone wrong. And He wants you to be like Him. God doesn't care where you lived as a child, or where you live now. God doesn't think a degree from one university is better than a degree from another, or that a college degree is better than no college degree. He doesn't rank us, and so there is no need to feel the need to impress Him. God loves to use people society has written off. He loves to take the ordinary and do something extraordinary. God wants to redeem your past so He can use you in truly significant, eternal ways. He wants to use your weakness to startle and amaze the so-called wise and qualified. After a laundry list of unthinkable sins, the apostle Paul wrote to the Christians in Corinth, saying, "And that is what some of you were. But you were washed, you were sanctified, you were justified in the name of the Lord Jesus Christ and by the Spirit of our God" (1 Corinthians 6:11). God loves to use our past to show the world His mercy.

My wife and I planted a small garden in the backyard of our first home. We planted corn, tomatoes, lettuce, cucumbers, squash, and okra. It was fun to walk outside in the summer evening and pick a fresh salad, but after one year we decided going to the grocery store was not such a bad idea after all. It was a struggle to keep things alive, except in the back, right hand corner. In that spot of the garden the soil was dark and rich. Things grew better and bigger there than anywhere else.

Why? What was so special about the back, right hand corner? It was special because the previous homeowners had a dog pen in that section of the yard. The back right hand corner was the place the dogs deposited waste on a daily basis for years and years, and it was their daily deposits, over time, that made the ground fertile for growth. God really does have a sense of humor, doesn't He?

The world may say, "Same mess . . . different day"; but what the world calls dung, God calls fertilizer. God turns trials into triumphs, defeats into victories, sadness into joy, and dysfunctions into destiny. He specializes in using the useless, loving the loveless, turning the ordinary into the extraordinary. If the situation you are presently in drives you to your knees and causes you to turn to Him, trusting Him more, guess what? God has you right where He wants you.

Your heavenly Father knows what He is doing. You were not an accident. He has not forgotten you, and neither has He forsaken you. God desires to use you, and your circumstances, to bring Him honor and glory. He can take your background and use it to build something beautiful in your life, and He can take your battle scars and bring about blessing.

21

## ENDNOTES

[1]Matthew 1:1-17; Luke 3:23-38.

[2]Matthew 1:3.

[3]Matthew 1:5.

[4]Matthew 1:6.

[5]It is a common mistake to confuse Palestine, Galilee, and Nazareth. Think of the three in terms of largest to smallest. Palestine refers to the entire land of Israel. Galilee refers to the northern province of Palestine. (Palestine consists of three provinces: Galilee, Samaria, and Judea.) Nazareth was a small town in the province of Galilee, in the land of Palestine.

[6]Peter was from Galilee, and it was his accent that gave him away. The Bible says, "Now Peter was sitting out in the courtyard, and a servant girl came to him. 'You also were with Jesus of Galilee,' she said . . . . After a little while, those standing there went up to Peter and said, 'Surely you are one of them, for your accent gives you away'" (Matthew 26:69, 73).

[7]Leviticus 12:1-8.

[8]The possibility that Joseph died when Jesus was a young boy, or teenager, and that, as the oldest son, Jesus was responsible for helping his mother take care of His brothers and sisters, may explain why Jesus waited until He was 30 to begin His public ministry. Another explanation is that it was customary for a Rabbi not to call disciples until he was 30 years of age.

[9]Trula Cronk's story is based on her autobiography, *Over Mountain or Plain or Sea*. (2003. Randall House Publications. Nashville, TN.) In October of 1984, the orphanage in Greenville, Tennessee was renamed the Trula Gunter Cronk Home for Children.

[10]Trula Cronk (pp. 212 and 216).

[11]1 Timothy 1:15.

# Questions for Discussion

1. Why do people allow their family's heritage—good, bad, and ugly—to determine their future?

2. What were the advantages of Jesus being born in the circumstances surrounding His birth? What were the disadvantages?

3. List ways in which a person's social ranking can affect that person's health, education, self esteem, or opportunities? How does that compare with what God says in Amos 5:11-12; Psalm 10:1-4; and James 5:1-6?

4. Why do you think our society judges others based on what they have, or where they are from, or who their parents were?

5. Have you ever thought you were an accident? Why did you think that? Do you still struggle with the idea that you were an accident? How did you overcome that thinking?

6. How does using people, who others consider unusable, bring glory to God? Give a modern day example of this?

7. God loves to use our past to show His mercy. How is this true in your life? Read 1 Corinthians 6:9-11. How do those verses apply to your life?

8. What do you feel is God's plan for your life?

# 3 The Time Is Now, but Not Yet

Every parent, especially first time parents, can't wait to return home after the birth of their child. However, instead of returning home after the birth of Jesus, Joseph and Mary fled to Egypt to live with a group of Jews near Alexandria. They went because an angel told them Herod was going to kill the Baby. A few years after their move to Egypt, Herod died.

Imagine the following conversation between Mary and Joseph as they prepared to leave Egypt.

"Is that everything?" Joseph asked as he secured the wagon carrying their belongings.

"Yes, I think so," came Mary's anxious reply. "Are you sure it is safe to go back home?" Is Herod really dead?"

Once again Joseph relayed the events of the last few days. "The other day," he said, "while working on a house in Alexandria, I overheard the homeowner, a high ranking official in the city, talk in great detail about how Herod had died. He said that his death was horrible.[1] He said that among other things, Herod suffered from muscular weakness, an intolerable itch, strong stomach pains, swelling around the feet, spasms, fainting, and difficulty in breathing. In fact, just a few days before his death, Herod tried to commit suicide with a knife! The only reason he did not succeed was because his cousin, Achiab, screamed for help.[2]

"My first thought was that he got what was coming to him. But God immediately reminded me of His words in the Torah: 'It is mine to avenge; I will repay. In due time their foot will slip; their day of disaster is near and their doom rushes upon them' (Deuteronomy 32:35). I immediately asked God to forgive my vengeful heart."

"How do we know these reports are true?" asked Mary.

"The homeowner, whom I overheard, has a friend who knows Nicolaus of Damascus, a close confidant of Herod. But that's not all, Mary," Joseph continued. "On the very night before I heard of Herod's death, an angel came to me in a dream and said, 'Get up, take the child and his mother and go to the land of Israel, for those who were trying to take the child's life are dead' (Matthew 2:20). At first I didn't think too much of the dream. But after I heard the news, I knew God had spoken".

Looking her straight in the eye, Joseph said, "Mary, with the same certainty the angel gave me to marry you and come to Egypt, he is now telling us to return home."

Mary knew from the look in his eyes and the passion in his voice that Joseph had heard from the Lord. She was tired of living the life of a refugee. She was ready to return home. Everyday, for three years, she had felt like a stranger in a strange land. She looked forward to being close to family and friends. She prayed their judgmental looks would be replaced with love and acceptance.

The journey was long, but the young family finally arrived in Galilee and settled in the small village of Nazareth. Joseph's carpentry skills landed him a good job. Mary enjoyed being a mother, watching her Son learn to walk and talk and play with the other children in the village.

The highlight of the year for a Jewish family was the Passover Feast, which was a celebration of God's deliverance of the Israelites from Egypt. The Passover commemorated the night the Hebrew people smeared the blood of the lamb on their doorposts as a signal to God to "pass over" the destruction that would happen on the homes without the blood. Each year, if at all possible, Jewish families traveled to Jerusalem to worship in the temple during this sacred event.[3] Herod[4] the Great, in an effort to ap-

Herod was hated by the Jews, and he knew it. The Jewish historian, Josephus, reports that a few days before his death, Herod called a group of beloved Jewish leaders to his bedside. As soon as they arrived he had them imprisoned. Afraid that no one would mourn his death, Herod gave orders that when he died, his death should be kept secret until the imprisoned Jewish leaders were killed. Following the announcement of the murders, his death was to be announced, insuring there would be crying throughout the empire. Fortunately, his orders were disobeyed, and the Jewish leaders were released, unharmed, after Herod's death.

pease his Jewish subjects, rebuilt the temple, and he spared no expense. He started the construction project in 19 B.C., but his successors did not finish the project until A.D. 64; and then the Roman army completely destroyed it in A.D. 70. The temple was made of white stone and gold that shone so brightly in the sun it was impossible to look at directly.

There was nothing quite like worshiping in the temple. There was nothing quite like the grandeur, pomp, and circumstance surrounding this glorious place. There was nothing quite like being in Jerusalem. The sight of so many people—some say as many as a million people—all gathered in once place, at the same time, for the same reason. The sounds of trumpets and singing and prayers. The smell of food and incense and burnt animals. All these things made the experience of going to Jerusalem to worship in the temple overwhelming.

Every year, Jesus and His family made the 80-mile, three-day journey from Nazareth to Bethlehem.[6] On one such trip, when Jesus was 12, He did not immediately return with His family. Because they traveled in large caravans for protection, Mary and Joseph did not notice Jesus' absence until they were a day removed from Jerusalem. After another day of looking for Him among the travelers, His parents spent a third day walking back to Jerusalem, where they found Jesus "sitting among the teachers, listening to them and asking them questions" (Luke 2:46).[7] The "teachers," known as "rabbis," taught using a question-and-answer format. Jesus, in asking questions, was also teaching the teachers. During this exchange, which apparently had been going on for a few days, people gathered

The Jewish historian, Josephus, wrote quite a bit about the beauty and majesty of the temple. On one occasion he wrote, "Now the exterior of the building wanted nothing that could astound either mind or eye. For, being covered on all sides with massive plates of gold, the sun was no sooner up than it radiated so fiery a flash that persons straining to look at it were compelled to avert their eyes as from solar rays. To approaching strangers it appeared from a distance like a snow-clad mountain; for all that was not overlaid with gold was of purest white ... Some of the stones in the building were forty-five cubits in length, five in height and six in breadth.[5]

around and were amazed and astonished at the young boy's questions and answers. It was clear to everyone present there was something different about Him. His time had come! He was a rabbinical prodigy. He was destined for great things. He was a boy wonder. Yet, right when things were starting to come together for Him, at the moment it seemed His

> *Yet, right when things were starting to come together for Him, at the moment it seemed His time had come, things came to a grinding halt. In truth, His time had not yet come.*

time had come, things came to a grinding halt. In truth, His time had not yet come. Mary and Joseph took Jesus home. It would be years before Jesus was heard from again.

Had Jesus jumped the gun in youthful exuberance? I don't know. But I do know Jesus returned to Nazareth with Mary and Joseph, and was obedient to them as His parents. During this time He also "grew in wisdom and stature, and in favor with God and men" (Luke 2:52). Nothing else is recorded in the Bible about Jesus until He is 30 years old.

But why? If Jesus was truly sent by God for a specific reason, why did He have to wait 30 years? If, at the age of 12, He was already amazing people with His teaching, why not start His ministry? How many more people could have been healed if His ministry would have started when He was 12, 18, or even 21? Why 30 years? That seems like such a long time!

## Follow . . . but Not Now

Have you ever felt like God has something definite and big for your life? Have you ever been frustrated because you knew God had a specific reason for creating you, and there is so much more in life than what you have experienced? Have you ever stepped out in faith to follow God, only to be jerked—like a dog out-running his leash—back into reality? Have you ever tried to walk through what you thought was an open door, only to discover it was a brick wall? Have you ever felt like God was saying to follow Him, and when you said, "Yes," He said, "Not now; go home and wait?"

It's discouraging, isn't it? It's a horrible feeling to want so much more, yet be in a position to have to wait. It's a horrible feeling to have to keep working that dead-end job, or stay in that isolated place of ministry, being obedient until some unknown time in the future. It's no fun watching other people soar, while you are stuck.

My responsibility, and your responsibility, during these times of waiting, is to grow and mature both in our faith and in our relationships with other people; that is what Jesus did. "Waiting" is an active verb, not a passive verb, when you are waiting on God.

> *My responsibility, and your responsibility, during these times of waiting, is to grow and mature, both in our faith and in our relationships with other people.*

Some people, who feel called by God for a certain task, will never see the promise fulfilled, at least not in this life. God considers such people, who walk by faith by constantly waiting, as true heroes. The writer of Hebrews wrote, "Now faith is being sure of what we hope for and certain of what we do not see . . . All these people were still living by faith when they died. They did not receive the things promised; they only saw them and welcomed them from a distance. And they admitted that they were aliens and strangers on earth. People who say such things show that they are looking for a country of their own. If they had been thinking of the country they had left, they would have had opportunity to return. Instead, they were longing for a better country—a heavenly one. Therefore God is not ashamed to be called their God, for he has prepared a city for them" (Hebrews 11:1, 13-16).[8]

## Follow . . . But First Go Deeper into the Desert

Jesus knew who He was. He knew what God had planned, and He was ready to get started fulfilling His purpose, but He was told to go back home and wait and grow and mature . . . and be tempted.

Eighteen years later, at the age of 30, Jesus journeys into the desert for a divine appointment with His cousin, John the Baptist. John came "baptizing in the desert region" (Mark 1:4). A better word for "desert" is "wilderness," and the Jordan River, where John baptized Jesus, ran through the wilderness.

After John baptized Jesus, a voice came from heaven saying, "You are My Son, whom I love; with You I am well pleased" (Mark 1:11). Surely now His time had come! But no, not yet, Jesus must first go deeper into the desert, deeper in the wilderness, deeper into complete isolation. Why? So He could be tempted by Satan.

The Bible says, "At once [immediately after His baptism] the Spirit sent him out into the desert, and he was in the desert forty days, being tempted by Satan. He was with the wild animals, and angels attended Him" (Mark 1:12-13). So deep did Jesus hike into the desert that His only companions were wild beasts. In the desert, Jesus was tempted in every way you and I are tempted.[9]

Before we get back to the story, let's examine what it means to say Jesus was tempted in the same ways that you and I are tempted.

Every temptation a person faces falls into at least one of three categories—pleasure, pride, and power. The Bible teaches us that everything "in the world—the cravings of sinful man [pleasure], the lust of his eyes [pride] and the boasting of what he has and does [power]—comes not from the Father but from the world" (1 John 2:16). When Satan tempted Jesus, his first temptation would have satisfied a physical desire Jesus had, namely hunger.[10] This falls under the category of pleasure. Next, Satan tempted Jesus' pride by reminding Him how important He was to God.[11] Finally, Satan offered Jesus "all the kingdoms of the world;"[12] an obvious temptation toward power. Thus, Jesus was tempted in every way you and I are tempted, yet He did not sin.

Now, back to the story.

Jesus' ministry did not get off to a smooth start. Every time it seems He is ready to go, God puts it off for a little longer. It makes no sense to us to postpone Jesus' work. Why did God keep putting obstacles in Jesus' path? Why does

God keep putting obstacles in our paths? He did it to Jesus, and He does it to us, because there are important lessons to be learned in waiting. God wants us to spend time in the desert, in the wilderness, in isolation so we learn to be completely dependent on Him.

We don't like the desert; it seems like such a waste of time. But God is quite fond of the desert. After 400 years of slavery, God used Moses to call His people out into the desert. Elijah fled into the desert to escape King Ahab. In the desert, ravens brought him food to eat, while he drank from a stream.[13] John the Baptist called people out into the desert to receive deliverance from their sins. Jesus goes deep into the desert to do battle with Satan.

Life is full of desert experiences. Maybe, right now, you are in the desert. You are stuck in a situation in

> *God likes the desert because in the desert is where you experience deliverance.*

which there seems no way out, with Satan tempting you at every turn. Do you feel isolated? Are you frustrated and ready to quit? Has sickness gotten the better of you, or have you experienced one failure after another? The desert is not a fun place to be, but it is a necessary part of your journey, following God. Hang in there. There is hope. God likes the desert because in the desert is where you experience deliverance.

When Moses returned to Egypt to ask Pharaoh to let the Israelites go, he said it was so they could go into the desert to worship God.[14] Jesus went into the wilderness to be tempted by Satan, and at the end of the 40 days of temptation, Matthew tells us "angels came and attended him."[15] Another word for "attended" is "ministered." No doubt part of their *ministering* to Jesus included *worshiping* Him. God still calls people into the desert to worship Him. In the desert there are few distractions. In the desert I can focus on God and depend on God and pray to God, like I never can in the busyness and success of life. After Jesus' encounter with Satan in the desert, the gospels tell us time and again that Jesus journeys back into the desert to be alone with

God. There is something about being alone with God, in the desert, worshiping Him, that energizes us to continue the journey.

Do you feel like you are alone in the desert? Do you feel dry and parched? Does it seem God has abandoned you? Be encouraged. Even if you feel like you are in the desert, all alone, God has not abandoned you, whether you are in the desert because of something you have done, or others have done to you, or because God has brought you there. Trust in Him and His timing. Maybe He has pushed you deep into the desert so you can be alone with Him to worship Him. As you worship God in the desert, regardless of the reason you are there, your strength will be renewed and you will be filled with grace, mercy, and hope. So, don't hurry to get out of the desert. Take advantage of it and soak up the warm sunshine of God's love.

> *It is in the desert, as you worship, that your strength is renewed, and you are filled with grace, mercy, and hope.*

But stay on guard. While desert experiences can bring you closer to God, the desert can also be a dangerous place. Only Mark mentions that Jesus was in the desert with "wild animals" (Mark 1:16).[16] Following God into the desert may cost you your life. It most certainly will cost you your dreams and aspirations. Following Jesus is following Him to the cross, and that's dangerous. Yes, the rewards are worth it. The promise of abundant, eternal life is real. But before you decide to follow God, you have to count the cost.

God likes the desert because it can be a place of deliverance, a place of worship, a place of testing, and a place of adventure. But maybe, the main reason God is fond of the desert is because the desert is where we spend most of our lives. The Israelites were delivered from their bondage—the past; but it would be years before they entered the Promise Land—the future. It was in the desert—the present, where they lived their lives. And God was with them in the desert! He was with them through the failures and through their

> *Maybe, the main reason God is fond of the desert is because the desert is where we spend most of our lives.*

sins and through the ups and downs and good and bad of their lives.

The moment you asked Jesus to come into your life and forgive you of your sins, you were delivered from your bondage; but that is in the past. As a follower of Jesus Christ you have the promise of a future hope; but that has not yet come. Right now you are caught in the present—the desert—and God is with you in the desert! You have not been called to live out your faith in the past. Neither have you been called to live out your faith in the future. You have only been called to live out your faith in the here and now—in the desert; facing the dangers, facing the testing, worshiping God because He has delivered you from your sins.

Being like Jesus means being pushed deep into the desert. It means following God in the here and now, and to walk with Him in the everyday, hard reality of life. It means having to wait, and it means having to overcome obstacles. Success is not having paradise on earth. Success is being set free from your past and given the strength you need to live in the present while you "wait for the blessed hope—the glorious appearing of our great God and Savior, Jesus Christ" (Titus 2:13).

## Caught Between Two Worlds

You and I live between two worlds. Jesus' message was that "the kingdom of God is near."[17] The kingdom of God is both now and not yet. This in between time is the desert in which we live. And that is not a bad thing. This world is not our home. It is, however, the desert through which we all must pass. And it is in this desert that we have been delivered from our sins, have the opportunity to worship almighty God, have the opportunity to build our faith through testing, and have the opportunity to see God's hand keep us safe through dangers.

It was only after Jesus journeyed out of the desert that His time to make a difference had come. It wasn't the night He was born. It wasn't in the temple when He was 12, and it wasn't immediately following His baptism. From a human perspective, things did not get off to a great start for Him. But from God's perspective, He would need all those experiences to fulfill His ministry; and time and again, Jesus voluntarily returned to the desert to be with God.

Your journey and my journey will be the same as His. Many times it will only be after you have journeyed out of the desert that God can really use you to do incredible, miraculous things. You may feel like your time is now, but maybe God is saying, "not yet." Regardless, trust in His sovereignty. Spend your time growing closer to Him, so that when your time does come, you will be ready to do incredible things for Him and His glory.

# ENDNOTES

[1] Among other things, doctors and historians have theorized that Herod died of poisoning, heart failure, kidney failure, some type of sexually transmitted disease, cancer, and or terminal edema of the lungs. He was 70 years old.

[2] The conversation between Mary and Joseph is imaginative. However, the symptoms that led to Herod's death are based on the Jewish historian, Josephus, account in his *Antiquities* 17.164-184.

[3] In actuality, there were three times each year when Jewish males were expected to travel to Jerusalem to worship in the temple: the Passover, Pentecost, and the Feast of Tabernacles.

[4] "Herod" was a title as much as a name. It was Herod the Great who wanted to kill the baby Jesus. After he died his sons became ruler. One of those sons, the most prominent one mentioned in the gospels, was Herod Antipas.

[5] Josephus, *J.W.* 5.5.6 (222-224).

[6] A more direct route would have been less than 80 miles, but that route went through Samaria. Because of the bad relationship between the Jews and Samaritans, Jesus' family would have taken the longer route. Luke 2:41 states, very clearly, that Jesus and His family made this journey every year. Because of Mary and Joseph's dedication to God, they made the trip every year This holy trip was made in spite of their limited resources to do so, and in spite of the fact, according to Mosaic Law, only males were required to attend each year.

[7] The whole story of this particular trip to Jerusalem and the temple is found in Luke 2:41-52.

[8] Hebrews 11:1, 13-16.

[9] Furthermore, Mark's Gospel never brings a close to Jesus' temptation like the other Gospel writers do. This suggest that from Mark's perspective, the dessert temptation was just one example of Jesus' battles with Satan. From Mark's perspective, Jesus was continually harassed and tempted, just like you and I, and He always overcome, just like you and I can do.

[10] Matthew 4:1-4.

[11] Matthew 4:5-7.

[12] Matthew 4:8-10.

[13] 1 Kings 17:1-6.

[14] Exodus 5:1; 8:1; 9:1, 9:13; 10:3 and others.

[15] Matthew 4:11.

[16] Mark 1:13.

[17] Mark 1:15.

# Questions for Discussion

1. Why do you think Jesus had to wait until He was 30 before He started His public ministry? What would have been the pros and cons of starting earlier?

2. Do you think it is possible for people to follow God, but "jump the gun" on entering ministry or starting a new ministry in church? Can you think of examples?

3. Why is it so hard to wait on God?

4. A lot of time was spent in this chapter on talking about "desert experiences." What do you think Riggs' meant by stressing the importance of desert experiences?

5. There were several reasons given in the chapter for why God allows desert experiences in our lives. Which one did you think was the most important?

6. How was Jesus tempted in every way, just like we are?

# 4    You Can't Go Home Again

"You can't go home again." At least that's what they say. I don't know if that is always true, and I don't know who "they" are, but I do know Jesus experienced the reality of that statement. Luke, the historian, records, "Jesus returned to Galilee . . . . He went to Nazareth, where he had been brought up" (Luke 4:14, 16). Before looking at the story of His return, I have to ask myself, "Where did Jesus go?"

According to the story, Jesus had just returned home from His baptism and desert temptation;[1] but I think there is more to the narrative than that. Luke writes, "and on the Sabbath day he went into the synagogue, as was his custom. And he stood up to read. (Luke 4:16).[2] Not just anyone was allowed to read and make comments in the synagogue. Only a teacher (or rabbi) was permitted to do so. At some point in His life, Jesus left home a carpenter's son and returned a rabbi.

How did that transition take place? How did Jesus become a rabbi? Why did He announce His ministry in the synagogue? Why did His hometown reject Him?

## From *Bet Sefer* to *Beth Midrash* to *Talmid* to *Rabbi*

The Torah[3] was everything to the Jewish people. Education meant survival, and so, central to their survival was Torah education. Jesus would have begun His formal training in the Torah at age 6. His first level of training, called *bet sefer* (meaning "house of the book") would last until he was 12 years of age (similar to our elementary school). During *bet sefer*, Jesus would have gone to school at the local synagogue and would have been taught by the *hazzan*, or the local rabbi ("Torah teacher"). A large part of the educational process was memorizing the Torah. In Jesus' day, most Jewish adults knew most of the Old Testament by heart.

At age 12, Jesus would have begun studying the oral interpretations of the Torah. At this stage of His education, question-and-answer times between student and teacher were common.[4] Between the ages of 13-15, gifted students were chosen from among the boys to continue their studies with a local rabbi in *beth midrash* (meaning "house of study," similar to our secondary schools). Those boys who were not chosen would return home to learn the family business. Assuming Jesus was chosen to continue His studies, during *beth midrash* He would have learned to apply the Torah and oral traditions to every day life.

From *beth midrash* were chosen the truly gifted students to travel and study with a famous rabbi as a *talmid* (meaning "disciple"). During this time in His life, Jesus would have left home to follow His rabbi anywhere the rabbi went. Around the age of 30, a *talmid* would be considered a "rabbi" and would begin His public ministry. And so, at the age of 30, Jesus returned home, to His synagogue, was recognized as a rabbi, and asked to read from the prophet Isaiah.[5]

## The Importance of the Synagogue

The synagogue[6] was the center of life for the Jewish community. The synagogue provided identity for the people and served as a place for school, public meetings, prayer, worship, court, and lodging for travelers. In Jesus' day, most Galilean towns had a synagogue. Outside the synagogue was a *mikveh* ("ritual bath") where people symbolically cleaned themselves before entering for worship. Once inside, along three walls, were "chief seats" where important people sat. Everyone else sat on the dirt floor. Teachers, speakers, and readers stood on the *bema* (a small platform), and on the bema was a small *menorah* (a candlestick like the one in the temple).

Every Friday evening, as soon as the first three stars could be seen, the *hazzan* blew the *shofar*, announcing the Sabbath had begun. Most families would gather for the Sabbath meal, and then go to the synagogue the following morning for worship. Worship in the synagogue included blessings, a recitation of the *Shema*,[7] and several readings

Do we know who Jesus' rabbi was? No, we don't. The Bible doesn't tell us. I am assuming He followed a rabbi based on the custom of the day. It is possible, but not likely, that He did not follow this custom. Here is what we do know:

By Jesus' day, most rabbis followed the teachings of one of two famous rabbis; Hillel or Shammai. Hillel, born around 65 B.C., died around A.D. 20, and was the more popular and liberal rabbi. By trade, Hillel was a woodcutter, and was known for his kindness, gentleness, and concern for humanity.

Shammai (date of birth and death unknown), a contemporary of Hillel and his key opponent, was a builder, known for the strictness of his views concerning the interpretation of Jewish law. After the death of Hillel, the followers of Shammai (known as Shammaites) controlled the Sanhedrin until the destruction of the temple in A.D. 70. Thus, the Pharisees whom Jesus encountered were strict Shammaites. Jesus' views were more closely aligned with Hillel's disciples (and more broadly accepted by the general populace), and would be another reason why the Pharisees despised Jesus so much. Below are but a few examples of the similarities between the teachings of Jesus and the teachings Hillel:

- Jesus—"For whoever exalts himself will be humbled, and whoever humbles himself will be exalted" (Matthew 23:12).
- Hillel—"My humiliation is my exaltation, my exaltation is my humiliation" (Lev. Rabbah, Chapt. 1).
- Jesus—"Give us today our daily bread" (Matthew 6:11).
- Hillel—"Give us each day our daily bread" (exact reference unknown).
- Both Jesus and Hillel taught the necessity of bringing the kingdom of heaven to the earth through revival and repentance.

from the Torah. The *hazzan* would have been the one to bring out the scrolls, but the passages to be read were assigned according to a predetermined schedule.

After the Torah readings, the prophets were read, followed by a short sermon on what the prophet said.[8] If a visiting rabbi was present, he would be asked to read from the prophets and share his thoughts on what it meant.

And so Jesus, who had returned home, was asked to read. By God's providence, when He was handed the scroll to read, the assigned text for the day was a prophecy about the coming Messiah from the prophet Isaiah. Because most of the people in the synagogue had most of the Old Testament memorized, they would know if Jesus were reading correctly.

Standing before His hometown friends and relatives, Jesus read, "The Spirit of the Lord is on me, because he has anointed me to preach the good news to the poor. He has sent me to proclaim freedom for the prisoners and recovery of sight for the blind, to release the oppressed, to proclaim the year of the Lord's favor" (Luke 4:18-19).[9]

In Jesus' day, the anticipation that a Messiah was soon coming was at a fever pitch. Thus, what Jesus read would have caused excitement, in and of itself. The fact this young, new rabbi was going to comment on these prophesies caused everyone to sit up straight and listen. Jesus' sermon, consisting of nine words, brought strong reactions. He startled them by saying, "Today, this scripture is fulfilled in your hearing" (Luke 4:21).

Jesus was claiming to be the Messiah! He was telling His family and friends, those who knew Him best and knew Him when, that He had been called by God to bring redemption and restoration to God's people.

How did the crowd react? "All the people in the synagogue were furious . . . . They got up, drove him out of the town, and took him to the brow of the hill on which the town was built, in order to throw him down the cliff" (Luke 4:28-29).

Not exactly what you would expect, or is it?

## A "Calling" from God

How do you explain a "calling" from God to your friends and family? What does it mean to say, "God has called me . . . ?" How do you know? How do you communicate your experience to others? The situation is especially complicated when you try to explain it to friends and family who do not follow Jesus, or who are not as committed to Him as you.

What does it mean to say you are "committed" to Jesus? Sometimes being committed means spending time in a psych ward. Is being "committed to Jesus" a fanatical, crazy idea?

I think some people like keeping their commitment to Jesus quiet, that way there is no accountability. I mean, if you tell someone of your intentions to do something great for

> The hazzan was the caretaker of the synagogue. He was responsible for maintaining the building and organizing prayer services. In smaller villages (like Nazareth) he taught the synagogue school. The hazzan would also announce the Sabbath by blowing the shofar (ram's horn); and he cared for the Torah scrolls and other sacred writings. (Visit www.followtherabbi.com to learn more about Jewish life in Jesus' day.)

Jesus, they will watch you closely and point out every flaw and misstep along the way. It's easier to keep some things between you and God, that way no one knows . . . except you and God. Why bring unnecessary attention to yourself? Why set yourself up for public humiliation?

Randy felt God calling him to be a minister when he was 15 years old. Actually, the first time he felt God calling, he was 12 years old; he was at a youth camp one summer during an emotional campfire service. Three years later, at age 15, he knew God was talking to him. But how could he tell and how could he explain it to others. Randy was a good kid, but he was known to swear once in a while; and he did other things that people, called by God, don't do. Who would believe him when he said, "God has called me to . . . ?"

One evening, Randy worked up the nerve to tell his dad how he was feeling and thinking. Surely his dad would understand because he also had been called by God into ministry. But his dad stunned him. He said, "Randy, if you can do anything else in life and be happy, do it."

What does that mean? Had God not called him? And there's that word again, *called*.

Several months passed, and Randy could not shake this feeling of being "called." One hot Sunday evening, he went before his church and announced that God had "called" him into ministry. The people at church—especially the older people—were thrilled. Randy, after all, was a good boy. Now all the adults watched him, hoping he would influence their sons and daughters. There is a lot of pressure in being "called."

A few months after his big announcement, Randy preached his first sermon. It was in children's church, and lasted ten whole minutes. He talked about baseball and the children loved him. "Maybe God has called me," he thought. Other speaking opportunities followed, and it seemed God had called Randy, but not everyone agreed. One pastor bluntly told him that God had not called him. But the "feeling" that God had "called" him would not leave.

What does it feel like to be "called"?

It's not the same feeling you have when you are cold, hot, or hungry. It's not something you can point to and say, "That's what it feels like." It's more like an inner knowing. It's something deep inside a person; something you cannot shake or escape. It keeps you up at night. It haunts you. It's something that says, "You will not be happy doing anything else."

Maybe, being "called" by God is not so much what God does, but how you respond to what God has already done, and is doing, in your life. If that's true, then we all have been called; it's just that very few have answered "yes."

> *It's easier to keep some things between you and God, that way no one knows . . . except you and God. Why bring unnecessary attention to yourself? Why set yourself up for public humiliation?*

What does it mean to be called by God? To be called by God means placing your life in God's hands, and not in the opinion of others. To be called by God means following Him, fulfilling His purpose in your life, even when other people question you; and at times, it is your friends and relatives, those who know you best, who cause you to doubt God's calling the most.

## Behold, the Lamb of God . . . I Think

On that day, after Jesus read from Isaiah in His home synagogue, the people did not believe Him, and so Jesus said, "No prophet is accepted in his hometown" (Luke 4:24). On another occasion, as people where crowding around Jesus, wanting His time and attention, His family came looking for Him, saying, "He is out of his mind" (Mark 3:21). Imagine that! Jesus thought He was called by God, but His family thought He was crazy. His friends wanted to kill Him.

How do you explain to your family that what you feel deep inside is what God wants you to do?

John the Baptist, Jesus' cousin, the one who baptized Him, said of Him, "Look, the Lamb of God, who takes away the sin of the world!" (John 1:29, 36). John knew God had called Him to go before the Messiah, preparing the way. He believed Jesus to be the Messiah. But then, from prison, John started doubting who Jesus was. John sent word to Jesus, asking, "Are you the one who was to come, or should we expect someone else?" (Matthew 11:3).

Sometimes, even our best friends doubt who we are, and who we claim to be.

Jesus was so good at being human it took awhile for people to believe He had been called by God to reconcile the world. He was so good at being human it was hard to believe He was God. For most of His family and friends, it took rising from the dead to convince them. And you know what? If someone in my family (like one of my brothers) claimed to be God's Son, it would take something no less dramatic than a resurrection to convince me. After all, I remember them when . . . .

The problem is that God still calls people who, like Jesus, are very good at being human. Moses was an orphaned child, who was guilty of murder, and whose only skill was being a shepherd. But God called Moses to deliver the

Herod Antipas had John the Baptist arrested and put in prison because John denounced his marriage to Herodias (Mark 6:17-18).

While on a visit to Rome to see his half-brother Philip, Herod fell in love with Philip's wife and proposed to her. Not only was Herodias his sister-in-law, she was also his half-niece. Her father was Herod's brother, and her mother was a sister of Herod the Great, Herod Antipas' father. The marriage between Herod Antipas and Herodias was adulterous and incestuous. And John told them so (Mark 6:18).

John the Baptist publicly denounced the marriage, which didn't sit well with the royal family. Before Herod could marry Herodias, Herodias asked him to divorce his wife, the daughter of Aretas IV, king of Nabatea. This humiliated Aretas IV, and military skirmishes started breaking out between the two provinces. John's preaching, thus, was politically explosive. So Herod had him arrested. Herodias wanted John killed, but Herod found him to be intriguing, so he "protected him, knowing him to be a righteous and holy man. When Herod heard John, he was greatly puzzled; yet he liked to listen to him" (Mark 6:19-20).

Israelites from bondage. Gideon was a timid farmer, with no dreams of being a military hero, but God called him to lead 300 men in one of the greatest military victories in history. There was nothing unusual about David, Daniel, Jeremiah, Deborah, Mary, or any of the apostles. Each was no more or no less human than you.

## Called by God

There are some things God calls everyone to do and be. God calls everyone to believe in Jesus. The Bible says, "The Lord is not slow in keeping his promise, as some understand slowness. He is patient with you, not wanting anyone to perish, but everyone to come to repentance" (2 Peter 3:9).

It is clear from Scripture and obvious from observation that not everyone will choose to believe, not everyone answers the call to faith, but that is God's calling nonetheless.

God also calls everyone to obey His teachings. Through His Word, God tells us what we need to know and what we need to do in order to live a fulfilled life. Through His Word we learn how to live and how not to live. The psalmist wrote, "Your word is a lamp to my feet and a light for my path" (Psalm 119:105).[10]

One of God's teachings is that we share our faith with others. Thus, another calling God has placed on everyone's life is to be an ambassador for Him. Further, God has called His followers to use their spiritual gifts in ministry.

> *Jesus was so good at being human it took awhile for people to believe He had been called by God to reconcile the world. He was so good at being human it was hard to believe He was God.*

There are other things God calls you to do, specifically, and no one else can do them like you. It is this unique calling that usually confuses us, and at times scares us. Unfortunately, we only apply this type of calling to being a pastor or a missionary. Yet, more often than not, in the Bible, when God calls a person, He calls them to something outside of ministry. The Scripture is full of examples where God called people to the marketplace, to build buildings (or a boat), to cut jewelry, to dig ditches, to take notes for someone else, to play music, to heal the sick, and to build roads.

I believe God still calls people. He calls some into ministry, but He calls most into some other type of life. God calls people to be a teacher, or a truck driver, or a doctor, or a Web site designer. To be called by God means to know without a doubt  what you are doing—whatever you are doing— is exactly what God wants you to be doing. God's calling is His personal invitation for you to get involved in building His kingdom by using your talents and gifts in significant, eternal ways. Answering God's call is completely submitting yourself to His will for your life. Thus, God's call is not about you, but about Him.

Bruce and Debbie felt God calling them to a specific place for a specific job. Bruce was a well-respected engineer at a nuclear plant—God had called him to be an engineer. They had a nice life with a nice home and two teenage children. But they felt called by God to leave their comfortableness behind and move to a third world country to help build a school. So Bruce quit his job, raised his support, and moved his family to a foreign country. Four years later, the school was built. They fell in love with the people in this South American country, but felt God calling them once again.

Where did God want Bruce and Debbie to go next? God was calling them back home! They struggled with this calling. What would other people think? Would they be labeled as quitters? But the call to return home was just as strong, and just as spiritual, as the call to move. The call to be an engineer was just as much a calling as the call to be a missionary. And not obeying that call would have been just as disobedient. Bruce is once again a respected engineer at a nuclear plant; and they are doing exactly what God wants them to do, where God wants them to do it. They have been called by God, and they have answered, "yes."

> *There are some things God calls everyone to do and be .... There are other things God calls you to do, specifically, and no one else can do them like you.*

## Is Anyone Home?

How do you know God is calling you?

If you are a living, breathing human being, God is calling you. He is calling you to faith in Jesus Christ. He is calling you to a higher life of obedience. He is calling you to share your faith and use your spiritual gifts. He is calling you to use your talents and skills for His honor and glory. As you answer God's call on these things, and open up the lines of your heart for further communications with the God of the universe, He will direct you to the specific calling or task He has for you.

How do you know you are living within that call? Athletes call it being in a "zone"; being in that place where the game slows down and you know you are in control. The fat part of a baseball bat is called the "sweet spot." Hit the ball there and it will go farther, harder, and faster than anywhere else on the bat. Living inside God's calling for your life is living in the "zone" or in the "sweet spot." It's a wonderful place to be; and when you are living in the zone, you know it.

How?

You know you are in the zone when there is a calmness in your soul that God is in control, regardless of the comfort or chaos going on around you. A person living within God's calling for his or her life is secure, satisfied, and content. Your heart is settled; you are able to live in the here and now without worrying about tomorrow; you are enjoying the journey. When you are in your "sweet spot" then you are joining God in what He is already doing, not begging Him to fit into your plans. The Bible calls living in the zone, abiding in Christ.[11]

When you know God has called you, you walk by faith, regardless of what anyone else says or thinks. There will be times in your journey following Jesus where people will question your motives, your competency, your calling, and even your sanity. At other times, people, who at one time believed in you and your calling, will start to doubt. More often than not, these doubters will be your friends and family, and church leaders. But when God has spoken into your heart, giving you a clear direction and calling, listen to Him. Obey Him. Press into Him. You will not be happy doing anything else.

And what if people oppose you? What if people stand in your way, or try to discourage you? Well, you do what Jesus did. In His hometown, His own people rejected Him and tried to kill Him. That is serious opposition! But Jesus "walked right through the crowd and went on his way" (Luke 4:30). Don't worry about what others think. When God has called you, don't let others—even family and friends—discourage you from obeying. Walk right through the opposition and continue on your way.

# ENDNOTES

[1]Luke 3.

[2]Notice that Luke says it was Jesus' custom to go to the synagogue on the Sabbath. Jesus was a faithful member of his "church."

[3]"Torah" means "teaching" or "way"; and refers to the first five books of the Old Testament. The Torah, Jews believed, was the very words of God.

[4]Remember when Jesus' parents found Him in the temple at age 12, He was both answering questions and asking questions. What He was doing was the customary way of learning and studying the oral interpretations of the Torah during *beth midrash.*

[5]Rob Bell does a masterful job painting a picture of what it meant to become a rabbi in his book, *Velvet Elvis,* chapter five, "Dust." I highly recommend you read this book. The story of Jesus returning home and reading from Isaiah, in the synagogue, is in Luke 4:14-22.

[6]The word *synagogue* means "assembly."

[7]The *Shema* was the basic confession of faith for a Jew. "Hear, O Israel: The LORD our God, the LORD is one. Love the Lord your God with all your heart and with all your soul and with all your strength" (Deuteronomy 6:4-5).

[8]The reading of the prophets was called "haphtarah"; and the short sermon was called "derashah."

[9]The quote was from Isaiah 61:1-2.

[10]Psalm 119:105.

[11]John 15:4.

# Questions for Discussion

1. How would you describe being called by God to others?

2. Why do you think the people reacted the way they did to the Jesus when He returned home?

3. "Maybe, being "called" by God is not so much what God does, but how you respond to what God has already done, and is doing, in your life. If that's true, then we all have been called; it's just that very few have answered "yes."? Rephrase that statement in your own words.

4. Discuss the things mentioned in this chapter that God has called everyone to do. List more things God has called everyone to do?

5. How can you know if and when God is really calling?

# 5        The "B" Team

I love the ocean. The breeze from the water, the smell of the sea, and the taste of the salt brings calmness over me that is hard to put in words. If you have experienced it, you know what I mean. I would choose the ocean over the mountains, swimming over hiking, any day.

Everyone needs a hobby. My hobby is scuba diving. I love the ocean, but I will dive in a fish pond. (I have been known to even dive in a baptistery.)

I once knew a guy who had a Ph.D. in something or other that told me the reason I am drawn to the sea is because I (like all life forms) came from the sea; and so my love for the ocean is a longing to return home. Some guys are so smart they make no sense.

I have a better explanation. I love the ocean because it reminds me of the power and creativity of God. The vastness of the sea preaches to me, proclaiming that God is bigger than I am, but He

In the Atlantic Ocean, 40 miles off the coast of Miami, Florida, south of Bimini, lies the great Bimini Wall. It faces the Gulf Stream, starts in 120 feet of water, and drops 1,000 or so feet straight to the bottom of the ocean. Scuba diving along the wall is an exhilarating experience. At about 80 feet, you swim through a beautiful choral reef system, full of aquatic life. Look carefully into the distance and you might see a hammerhead shark. At the edge of the reef is the beginning of the Wall. At 120 feet, you can look over the Wall, into total darkness. Looking down into the pit is one of the eeriest things I have ever done.

As I was looking over into that great chasm, it hit me. My sins are buried at the bottom! God lavished His love on me by sending Jesus to die on the cross so I could be forgiven. He has taken my sins and cast them into the sea of forgetfulness. I now have a visual picture of what that sea looks like. Not only are my sins at the bottom, so are yours.

still loves me and His grace is deeper than the deepest ocean canyon. My love for the ocean *is* a longing to go home, but not to some lower life form from which I came, but to my final destination, next to the Creator of the sea, in whose image I was formed.

There is a verse in the Bible I don't like. I accept it, but I don't like it. It's Revelation 21:1, "Then I saw a new heaven and a new earth, for the first heaven and the first earth had passed away [I like this part], *and there was no longer any sea*"(italics mine). I don't like that last part. Why no sea in heaven?

I also love to fish. I like all things related to the water. One day I hope to learn how to sail. My dream is to spend my retirement sailing the Intercoastal Waterways, scuba diving and fishing all along the way.

> *I think Jesus loved the ocean. I think He would have liked scuba diving; and apparently He had an admiration for boats and fishermen.*

I think Jesus loved the ocean. I think He would have liked scuba diving; and apparently He had an admiration for boats and fishermen. Jesus chose 12 young men to be His disciples. Six (possibly seven) of the 12 were fishermen by trade; two were civil servants; one was a carpenter; and the occupations of three are unknown.[1] Wow! Half of His first followers were fishermen!

Fishing in first century Palestine was hard work, and not very profitable, unless you could afford to purchase the "fishing rights" sold by the Herods. Those who owned the fishing rights would sublet the rights to actual fishermen, who did all the work and paid a hefty tax to the investors. Little love was lost between the fishermen and these investors, who were sometimes referred to as "tax collectors." Matthew (also known as Levi), one of the chosen Twelve, was a tax collector. It made little sense for Jesus to choose several fishermen, and a tax collector, to be His disciples.

The Sea of Galilee[2] could be considered the cradle of the gospel because of its prominence in the travels of Jesus. Jesus' adopted hometown, Capernaum, was on the northern shore. Close to Capernaum was the city of Bethsaida, meaning "house of fishing" or "fisherman's house." Bethsaida was the hometown of Peter, Andrew, and Philip. The city of Magdala,[3] located on the western shore, was the center of the fishing industry, and home of Mary Magdalene.[4]

An oval, fresh water lake, resting 682 feet below sea level,[5] the Sea of Galilee is 12 ½ miles long and 7 ½ miles wide at its widest; and ranges in depth from 80 feet to 200 feet. In Jesus' day, the Sea of Galilee abounded in fish, with more than 20 different species indigenous to the lake.

Fishing on the Sea of Galilee was mainly done at night and with nets. The "dragnet" (used for fishing) was the oldest type of net and took as many as 32 men to operate. The dragnet, shaped like a long wall, was typically 300 feet long and 12 feet high. Weights and sinkers were attached to the bottom of the net and corked floats were attached to the top. One team of 16 men would hold on to a strong rope attached to the dragnet. The boat would then sail out with another team until the net was fully stretched and then circled around and back to shore. A second team of 16 would hold ropes. Then, both teams would drag the nets, and its contents, back to the shore. Once on shore, the fish were sorted and the operation performed again, sometimes as many as eight times in one day or night of fishing. Clearly, fishing was hard work.

A much smaller net was the "cast net." About 20 feet in diameter, with weights of lead attached to the border, one man would throw the cast net in a circle, either from shore or from a boat. When the net hit the water, the weights

The oldest Christian symbol is the fish. The Greek word for fish, *ichthus*, was used as an acrostic by the earliest Christians. The translation of the acrostic was, "Jesus Christ Son of God Savior." The symbol of a fish was used as a code name for Christ by persecuted Christians in order to avoid arrest and execution by Roman authorities. If a picture of a fish appeared outside a Roman home it meant that night a group of believers would gather in that home for "church." Thus, throughout church history the fish symbol is seen in Christian art and literature. Next to the cross, the fish is the most revered symbol in Christian history.

would come together, trapping the fish inside. This was a popular way to fish, especially during the day, and was most likely the way some of the disciples were fishing when Jesus walked along the shore and asked them to follow Him.

At night, fishermen ventured out into deeper waters where they used a "trammel net" composed of two large mesh nets with a fine inner net in between. One end of the net would be lowered down, and then the boat would make a large circle. Unable to escape through the three layers of netting, the trammel net caught every kind of fish imaginable. After a night of fishing, the nets were spread out on the rocks to dry and be mended. Rarely, and only in emergencies, would the nets be mended on the boats. Yet, that is exactly what James and John were doing when Jesus called to them. They immediately left what they were doing—emergency or not—and followed Him.[6]

Fishermen were known as hard workers. They were blue-collar people who stuck together. They were also rough and rugged, both in their lifestyle and language. And although the fishermen Jesus chose to be His followers were devout Jews—and followers of John the Baptist—they still would have been typical fishermen of the day.

On one occasion, out of frustration, Jesus commented to His disciples that they were somewhat dense.[7] Like Jesus, His disciples would have followed the traditional formal education process of Jewish boys.[8] Beginning at age 6, and continuing until age 12, they would have gone to *bet-sefer*, where they would have memorized the Torah. All young boys completed this first phase of education. But only the most gifted would continue their education to the next level, *beth-midrash*. Only the most gifted after that level would have been chosen by a rabbi to be a disciple—*talmid*. The boys not chosen to continue past *bet-sefer* returned home to learn the family business. And that is exactly what happened to Peter, James, John, and Andrew and possibly some of the other disciples. They were not considered bright enough to continue any type of formal education. They were not considered smart enough, by others, to be anyone's disciples!

# The "B" Team

My daughter's junior high school, consisting of only eighth and ninth grades, was quite large. In order to give everyone an opportunity to participate in sports, the school was divided in half—West Side and East Side—and for sports, each side had an eighth grade team and a ninth grade team. Divided even more, each team (with the exception of football) had an "A" team and a "B" team. For example, in volleyball (Katherine's favorite) there was an eighth grade "A" team and an eighth grade "B" team for both East and West; a ninth grade "A" team and an ninth grade "B" team for both East and West. The best players were on the "A" teams. To be on the "B" team was just a notch above being "cut" from the team altogether. Even the uniforms for the "A" team were better. There wasn't much glory or fanfare in being on the "B" team. Logically, it made sense to have several teams of volleyball (and basketball), but realistically, it created a caste system and class envy. No one wants to be on the "B" team!

Jesus chose His disciples off the "B" team. When Jesus chose His followers, He did not choose those that the world thought to be the best and brightest! For the most part, He chose men that others had written off.

"A fact we cannot deny is that no body of men, few or many, has ever exercised so vast an influence on the world as the small circle of ordinary men Jesus called, trained, commissioned and empowered to further His cause. Surveyed from the human angle, the twelve had meager equipment for the great tasks before them. They are referred to as being 'unlettered and ignorant men,' which means they were unprofessional men absolutely outside the current schools of philosophical, political and religious thought . . . . If Christ could use the best of men, who were only men at best, then He can use us . . . . He chose peasants from the village, provincial townsmen, and toilers of the sea as His first disciples. While most of them earned their livelihood by ordinary handicrafts, and were evidently respectable men from the moral point of view, with a religious bent in their character, there was nothing about them to give one the slightest indication of exceptional qualities or fitness for the remarkable service they were to render . . . . The transformation of the twelve was not the least, it was almost the greatest of Christ's miracles" (Herbert Lockyer, *All The Apostles of the Bible*, Grand Rapids, MI: Zondervan Publishing House, 7-8, 11, 1972).

55

The only thing spectacular about any of the men Jesus chose was their extraordinary ordinariness. Not a single one of them was known for his communication styles, or his scholarship, or his organizational abilities. Instead, they were known for their outbursts, mistakes, arrogance, misstatements, bad attitudes, lapses of faith, and bitter failures.[9]

In God's eyes, there are no "B" teams.

> *God is not out to get you. He wants to restore you to Himself, transforming you into what you were meant to be in the first place.*

You were created in the image of God. Sure, you've made mistakes, and so have I . . . big ones! I have let God down, and so have you . . . lots of times. The image of God inside us may be distorted and disfigured, but it's still there waiting to bust out. God doesn't want to *change* you. He created you, and now He wants to *recreate* you into the image of His Son, Jesus Christ! God is not out to get you. He wants to *restore* you to Himself, transforming you into what you were meant to be in the first place. To use a computer analogy: *God wants to restore the factory setting in your life, getting rid of all the viruses, so you can run efficiently.*

God doesn't dwell on our past mistakes. He doesn't dwell on our past sins. He doesn't focus on our past failures or our past victories. God desires to focus on what you can be, not what you are, focusing on your potential, not on your present. Jesus loves and accepts you for who you are today and He sees the greatness in you that others cannot see—both now and in the future.

## What Jesus Looks for in Disciples

You don't have to look any further than the Twelve Jesus chose to see what it is He looks for in disciples. To prove my point, I want us to look briefly at the lives of the lesser known disciples. If the disciples were made up of "B" team players, these four were on team "C"—Thaddaeus, Simon, James, and Matthias.

# THADDAEUS

In Luke's list of disciples, Thaddaeus is identified as "Judas son of James" (Luke 6:16). Matthew refers to him as "Labbaeus, whose surname was Thaddaeus" (Matthew 10:3, KJV). More than likely, his given name was Judas (a common name in that day); Thaddaeus and Labbaeus were nicknames, with the name Thaddaeus sticking.

Nicknames are nothing more than names people call one another based on a person's characteristics. Sometimes nicknames represent a person's strength—Big Jim or Hulk Hogan. Sometimes nicknames tell us about a person's achievement or position—Doc, Coach, or Rev. A nickname could describe a physical characteristic—Red or Slim. Sometimes nicknames tell us about a person's character—Honest Abe. However, at times, nicknames can be hurtful—Klutzo, Dumbo, or Metal Mouth.

No matter the nickname, it often describes us better than our real names. Nicknames reveal something about who we are, or how others perceive us. Nicknames show other people our vulnerability.

As nicknames go, Thaddaeus was not good. Thaddaeus means "breast child" and Labbaeus means "heart child." Both would be similar to calling someone a "momma's boy." Thaddaeus must have been a gentle and meek individual, who was tenderhearted and sensitive, to receive such a nickname.[10]

What others saw as a weakness, Jesus saw as a tremendous strength. Jesus chose Thaddaeus when no one else would. Church tradition says Thaddaeus ministered to the north in Mesopotamia (modern day Turkey) where he healed Abgar, the king of Edessa.[11] Thaddaeus refused to renounce his faith in Jesus, and as a result was beaten to death with a club and then beheaded.

Vulnerability doesn't mean you wear your feelings on your sleeve or that you are a pushover. It doesn't mean you are easily upset by other people. No, to be vulnerable means to be real. It means you know your strengths and weaknesses and that you are comfortable with who you are and who

God created you to be. It means you are transparent—what you see is what you get—and that you don't operate with hidden agendas. The best advice concerning vulnerability is Romans 12:3, "For by the grace given me I say to every one of you: Do not think of yourself more highly than you ought, but rather think of yourself with sober judgment, in accordance with the measure of faith God has given you."

> To be vulnerable means to be real. It means you know your strengths and weaknesses, and that you are comfortable with who you are and who God created you to be.

## SIMON

Not a whole lot is known about Simon; however, one thing we do know—you never had to wonder where Simon stood or what he thought. If he was nothing else, he was *authentic* and *genuine*. How do I know? Because, like Thaddaeus he, too, had a nickname that speaks volumes. He wasn't just Simon. He was "Simon the Zealot" (Luke 6:15 and Acts 1:13).

In Jesus' day there were four political parties among the Jews: (1) the Pharisees—religious fundamentalists; (2) the Sadducees—religious liberals who denied anything supernatural; (3) the Essenes—ascetic celibates who lived in the desert, devoting their lives to studying the Old Testament; and (4) the Zealots—extremists who hated the Romans and hoped to overthrow the Roman occupation.

Apparently, at one time in his life, Simon was a member of the fourth political group.[12] People make a big deal about the brashness and temper of Peter, but Peter was tame compared to Simon. The Zealots advanced their agenda primarily through terrorism and acts of violence. Only God had the right to rule over them, and so they believed assassinating Roman soldiers, political leaders, and anyone else who opposed them, was doing God's work. Zealots were ready to fight and die for their patriotism.

Others would have seen Simon as a person too extreme, too violent to do any good. But Jesus saw in Simon a man of fierce loyalties, amazing passions, courage, and zeal. Church traditions have him preaching the gospel in Egypt, Persia, and the British Isles, giving his life for the message of Jesus by having his body mutilated.

To be authentic is the opposite of being hypocritical. To be authentic means you are a person of integrity. It means your life backs up what you believe. There is no disconnect between belief and behavior for the truly authentic person.

> *There is no disconnect between belief and behavior for the truly authentic person.*

## JAMES

There is no doubt Jesus prized *humility,* and the one disciple who shows us humility is James, son of Alphaeus. In church tradition he is known as "James the Lesser"—another, non-flattering nickname. He is known this way to differentiate him from the other disciple named James,[13] the brother of John. "Lesser" does not mean inferior or "not as important;" and could refer to his size (meaning he was small), or to his age (meaning he was young).

Nothing is said in the New Testament about James the Lesser; only his name is mentioned. Tradition says he was a humble man of fervent prayer. One tradition says he spent so much time on his knees in prayer that his knees thickened and looked like the knees of a camel. It is believed he took the gospel to Syria and Persia where he died by being beaten with a club and then sawed in pieces.

Humility is like underwear—necessary, but indecent if shown. Humility is the opposite of arrogance, but it is not the same thing as self-abasement. A humble person no more tears himself down as he builds him-

> *To be humble means to see yourself the way God sees you. You are a wonderful person, full of unique talents and abilities; but those talents and abilities come from God and will only reach their fullest potential in relationship to Him.*

self up. To be humble means to see yourself the way God sees you. You are a wonderful person, full of unique talents and abilities; but those talents and abilities come from God and will only reach their fullest potential in relationship to Him. Solomon, the wisest man ever, put it this way: "A man's pride brings him low, but a man of lowly spirit [humility] gains honor" (Proverbs 29:23).

## MATTHIAS

After Jesus' ascension, the disciples, along with 120 followers, returned to Jerusalem. While gathered with the whole group, Peter explained someone needed to be selected to take Judas Iscariot's place. Peter said, "Therefore it is necessary to choose one of the men who have been with us the whole time the Lord Jesus went in and out among us, beginning from John's baptism to the time when Jesus was taken up from us. For one of these must become a witness with us of his resurrection" (Acts 2:21-22). After a time of worship and prayer, Matthias was selected and "added to the eleven apostles" (Acts 1:26).

Out of the Twelve, Matthias was the most quiet and obscure. All we know is he was a loyal follower of Jesus, having been with Him as long as the others. He followed Jesus, faithfully waiting his turn, never forcing himself into the spotlight, never complaining, and always making himself available to serve. Tradition says he was martyred with a spear in southern Asia because he proclaimed Jesus as God.

It has been said that the best ability is availability, and that is what Matthias shows us. The only credentials he had were that he had always been willing and able to serve.

Making yourself available means more than being in the right place at the right time. Availability is an attitude that says, "I will do whatever needs to be done"; and it is a lifestyle that does whatever needs to be done.

Thaddaeus—tenderhearted and sensitive. Simon the Zealot—passionate and loyal. James the Lesser—a man of fervent prayer. Matthias—quiet and obscure. From these four individuals we learn that Jesus looks for vulnerability, authenticity, humility, and availability. And here is the punch line: *All of us can be those things!* We can't all be great and famous. Not all of us can preach, teach, write, sing, or be missionaries or whatever . . . . But we can all make ourselves vulnerable, authentic, humble, and available so Jesus can use us to change our world.

Another big lesson from these four ordinary guys is

that they were *individuals.* Each person was unique. Each person had strengths and weaknesses. Each man was a normal human being. But Jesus transformed them. Jesus took their strengths and weaknesses; He took their individuality; and He transformed them into *community.* By themselves they were powerless to change the world, but in community nothing in the world could stop them.

> *And here is the punch line: All of us can be those things! We can't all be great and famous. Not all of us can preach, teach, write, sing, be missionaries or whatever . . . . But we can all make ourselves vulnerable, authentic, humble, and available so Jesus can use us to change our world.*

Every one of us must come to Christ as individuals, but immediately we are called to live our faith in community. God desires to take our uniqueness, gifts, talents, strengths, and weaknesses and blend them together in community to do a great work for Him.

## ENDNOTES

[1]The six fishermen were Peter, Andrew, James, John, Philip, and Nathanael. The two civil servants were Alphaeus and Matthew (a tax collector also known as Levi). Thomas was a carpenter; and the occupations of Simon, Jude (also known as Bar Jacob), and Judas Iscariot are unknown. Also, the occupation of Matthias, who replaced Judas, is unknown.

[2]Besides being called the Sea of Galilee, the Bible also refers to this large fresh water lake as the Sea of Kinnereth (Numbers 34:11; Joshua 12:3; 13:27), the Lake of Gennesaret (Luke 5:1), and the Sea of Tiberias (John 6:1; 21:1).

[3]The name *Magdala* is Hebrew, meaning "tower," suggesting that the city was the site of a guard tower overlooking an important trade route. The Greek name for the city was *Tarichaea,* meaning "dried fish." Here, the fish would be packed in baskets for export. Fishermen would then take the dried fish by mule-drawn wagons to shops in Jerusalem or to a seaport where they would be loaded on ships and taken to Rome. Dried fish from Galilee was considered a delicacy among the Roman elite.

[4]"Mary Magdalene" means "Mary of Magdala." It is quite possible that Mary Magdalene was from a wealthy, prominent family in Magdala.

[5]The only body of water lower than the Sea of Galilee is the Dead Sea. The Jordan River runs through the Sea of Galilee and empties into the Dead Sea.

[6]The story of James and John is found in Matthew 4:21-22. I found some helpful information about fishing from an article written by Dr. Elizabeth McNamer, in the July, 2004 edition of "Scripture From Scratch."

[7]Luke 24:25.

[8]A more detailed explanation of the education process is found in chapter 4.

[9]Two excellent books on the life of the apostles are John MacArthur's book, *Twelve Ordinary Men;* and Gene Getz's book, *The Apostles: Becoming Unified Through Diversity.* I highly recommend both.

[10]The names *Thaddaeus* and *Labbaeus* could also refer to him being the youngest among several siblings.

[11]Eusebius, a 4th century historian, wrote that the archives at Edessa (now destroyed) contained full records of Thaddaeus' visit and the healing of Abgar.

[12]Some scholars believe Judas Iscariot was part of the Zealots as well. When Jesus sent the disciples out two-by-two, it is probable that Simon and Judas paired up.

[13]Known in church history as "James the Greater."

# Questions for Discussion

1.  What characteristics of fishermen do you think Jesus liked that caused Him to choose fishermen to be His disciples? What do those characteristics say about us?

2.  Was there a time in your life where you were placed on the "B" team, or demoted to second place? How did it make you feel? How did you handle it? Have you ever felt like second place in your relationship with Christ?

3.  What does Jesus look for in disciples? Of the qualities He looks for mentioned in this chapter, which one do you think is your strength and which one do you think is your weakness? Why?

4.  Of the four lesser disciples mentioned in this chapter, which one do you relate to the most? Why?

5.  Even though we come to Christ as individuals, we are called to live out our faith in community. How do we live out our faith in community?

# 6

# Some Say He
# Was an Outlaw

"He was not Jesus of Nazareth, the Son of God! He was Jesus, the bastard child of Mary and Pantera, a Roman soldier. He was not the Messiah! He was a troublemaker, a rebel, a criminal, an outlaw. That is why He was executed!"

Not long after Jesus' death, His opponents tried to discredit Him by spreading such a rumor.[1] The idea would have been preposterous, except Roman soldiers raping Jewish girls was something that happened far too often, especially in a small town like Nazareth.

The rumor about Mary and a Roman soldier named Pantera tells us something about the political situation into which Jesus was born.

## Revolts, Revolutions, and Rebellions[2]

After his death in 323 B.C., Alexander the Great's empire was divided among his generals. Israel (or Palestine) fell under the control of Seleucus, who quickly developed a heavy system of taxation making life difficult for the Hebrews. At times, the tax system took as much as 33 percent of a person's income.

In addition to keeping the heavy taxes, in 167 B.C. Antiochus IV Epiphanes outlawed the Torah, the practice of circumcision, the observance of Jewish dietary laws, and the Jewish sacrificial system. Antiochus set himself up as God,[3] ordering the Israelites to forsake worshiping their God for the worship of himself and Zeus. The key element in this "new" worship was sacrificing a pig on the holy altar.[4] Soldiers were stationed throughout Israel to enforce compliance and squash rebellion.

One man and his sons in the small Judean town of Modein refused to comply. Mattathias and his six sons attacked the soldiers, leading a rebellion against them. The oldest son, Judas, became the leader of the revolt and was given the name *Maccabeus*, meaning "hammer." This rebellion, known as the "Maccabean Revolt," came to a climax in 164 B.C. when the Maccabean Freedom Fighters liberated Jerusalem. Twenty-two years later (142 B.C.), after a generation of grueling guerrilla warfare, the last occupiers left Israel. The Jewish holiday, Hanukkah, celebrates this liberation.

With the occupiers gone, the Jews were "free"[5] for the first time since 597 B.C.[6] They formed their own government and dreamed of their messiah coming to reinstate the reign of King David. Yet, skirmishes continued between the Jews and the Greeks up to, and through, the time of Jesus. In 43 B.C., Cassius[7] conquered a town in Galilee, enslaving all 30,000 of its civilians. In 40 B.C. the Roman authorities gave control of Galilee to a half-Jew, half-Arab person who became known as Herod the Great. Herod ruled by terror, seizing Jerusalem around 37 B.C. Josephus, the ancient Jewish historian, describes the attack this way: "when the troops poured in, a scene of wholesale massacre ensued; for the Romans were infuriated by the length of the siege, and the Jews of Herod's army were determined to leave none of their opponents alive. Masses were butchered in the alleys, crowded together in the houses and flying into the sanctuary."[8]

By the time of Jesus' birth, political, racial, and ethnic tensions were rising. Even the New Testament mentions a skirmish that took place around 6 A.D.[9] Luke, the historian, writes: "After him, Judas the Galilean[10] appeared in the days of the census and led a band of people in revolt. He too was killed, and all his followers were scattered" (Acts 5:37).[11]

Judas, along with Zadok, led a group of Zealots against the Romans. Judas proclaimed the Jewish nation was not under the authority of Rome, but was a republic that recognized God alone as King and Ruler. Even after his death, his revolt continued to the point that his two sons, Jacob and Simon, were crucified by Tiberius. Another of his sons, Menahem, led a group of assassins called Sicarii—or, pronounced another way, Iscariot, of which Judas, the betrayer of Jesus, may have been a part.

Are you beginning to see the cultural turmoil into which Jesus was born? Faithful Jews were anticipating the arrival of their messiah; but their idea of the messiah was political—and even militant. As a result, the Roman authorities were looking and watching for troublemakers. The moment one appeared on the scene—if it seemed he was gathering a following—soldiers would pounce and put the movement to an end, often times crucifying the leader.[12]

Within Judaism itself, there were four groups vying for the people's allegiance. Each group had its own idea about the coming of a messiah and what the messiah would do. Jesus did not fit any of their ideas.

## PHARISEES

First, were the Pharisees. The Pharisees are objects of extreme criticisms by most modern-day believers, and rightfully so, but that wasn't always the case. At one time in their history the Pharisees were well respected in the Jewish community.

There is debate over the correct translation of "Iscariot." Some believe it simply refers to the town of Kerioth in southern Judah; thus, perhaps Judas was from Kerioth. However, others believe the word makes reference to "Sicarii," the most radical group of Jewish zealots known for their terrorist type attacks on the Roman government; thus, Judas could have been part of this group of radicals.

The Pharisees loved the Mosaic Law and took vows to keep every detail of the Law. The problem was their rules and regulations got in the way of their relationships with one another, the public, and ultimately with God. Keeping the Law became an end in itself instead of a means to an end.

The Pharisees had strong opinions about the coming of the messiah and the role he would play. They believed the messiah would set up his kingdom on earth, overthrow their Roman oppressors, and reestablish the kingdom of David. Thus, the messiah would be a political freedom fighter who would set up a monarchy, oftentimes referred by them as the "kingdom of God" (or "kingdom of heaven"). Instead of embracing Jesus as Messiah, the Pharisees accused Him of blasphemy.

One of Jesus' characteristics was that He was able to deliver people from demonic possession. After witnessing a series of such encounters, the Pharisees said of Him, "He is possessed by Beelzebub! By the prince of demons he is driving out demons" (Mark 3:22). On another occasion, after Jesus healed a paralyzed man, telling him his sins were forgiven, the Pharisees protested saying, "This fellow is blaspheming!" (Matthew 9:3).[14] And then, after He was arrested, Jesus was questioned by the Sanhedrin:[15] "The high priest said to him, 'I charge you under oath by the living God: Tell us if you are the Christ, the Son of God'" (Matthew 26:63-64). Jesus answered that He was. "Then the high priest tore his clothes and said, 'He has spoken blasphemy! Why do we need any more witnesses? Look, now you have heard the blasphemy. What do you think?'" (Matthew 26:65-66). Instead of embracing Him as God, they tried (and eventually succeeded) in alienating Him from people. It was the people whom Jesus came to redeem that yelled and screamed for Him to die![16]

> Religion[13] helps us connect with God in meaningful, authentic ways. When any religious practice (or ritual) keeps us from connecting with God, it should be changed, altered, updated, or dropped all together. To continue such a practice would be to elevate it from a means to an end in itself.
>
> For example: The order of our worship services, types of music we sing in worship, and the number of times a church meets each week are all designed to help us connect with God and should appropriately be changed, updated, and altered. When these things lose their meaning, and we continue to go through the motions, we do more harm than good.

It seems the main problem the Pharisees had with Jesus was that He emphasized keeping the spirit of the Law over keeping the letter of the Law—a revolutionary idea. Jesus taught you could do exactly what the Law commands, and still not be right with God! Jesus told the Pharisees that although they were physical descendants of Abraham, their real father was Satan.[17] Needless to say, that didn't sit well with them. The bottom line was Jesus placed people above procedures. He looked on the inward heart of a person, instead of the outward action. He placed relationship above ritual.

Sherry grew up, not only in a Christian home, but in a pastor's home. She was a good girl, nothing more than normal rebellion, never anything serious. After Sherry graduated from high school, she went to a Christian college in the northwest. After all, that's what was expected of a pastor's daughter. One night, while in college, Sherry got caught in the wrong place at the wrong time. It was a small party and it didn't last very long, but boys and girls were both present and alcohol was involved. College rules were broken. Another student turned her in. No grace was extended because, after all, rules are rules, and so Sherry was kicked out of school.

Since nothing like this had ever happened to her before, Sherry's college pastor went to the dean of the school on her behalf. Nothing changed. She would not be allowed back. Sherry had a good heart. She deserved another chance, but sometimes Pharisees can be irrational. "Letting a girl like her stay in school would harm the entire school's reputation," the dean told her pastor.

Sherry did not fit into other people's box of what a Christian should be and how a Christian should act! She loved Jesus, and wanted to follow Him, but she just didn't fit in to the traditional religious cookie-cutter like everyone else. She wasn't a troublemaker. She wasn't rebellious. Quite the contrary! She was passionate about life, about Christ, and about making a difference.

Sherry's college pastor never gave up on her. He encouraged her and loved her. During her time away from school, she grew and matured. Eventually she went back to school, graduated, and is now serving along side her husband in full-time ministry. While I completely understand that rules are intended to shape people and provide institutional boundaries for a community of students, I believe there should be latitude to correct; and often, expulsion removes that latitude and the opportunity to mentor. Sometimes people are more important than rules and institutional reputations.

## SADDUCEES

A rival group to the Pharisees was the Sadducees. The Sadducees were the aristocrats of Jewish society (or so they thought and acted). The Sadducees represented nobility, power, and wealth. As a result, they were not overly concerned with the hope of a coming messiah. Their aim was temporary wealth and worldly success. The messiah (if he actually ever came) would upset their lifestyle and their friendship with the Romans. Keeping the status quo was in their best interest.

More interested in politics than religion, the Sadducees did not believe in any type of resurrection or immortality of the soul. They only followed the Jewish Law when it was convenient, and would rather debate than pray. On more than one occasion, members of the Sadducees tried to argue with Jesus.

For example, following their bias, the Sadducees tried to entrap Jesus in a debate about the resurrection. The basis for their argument was a woman who had incredibly bad luck with husbands. This woman married seven different brothers at seven different times after each previous brother died, leaving her a widow…times seven. Finally, tired from burying so many husbands, the woman dies.

Sarcastically, the Sadducees asked Jesus, "Now then, at the resurrection, whose wife will she be of the seven?" (Matthew 22:28).[18]

In His response, Jesus accused them of being ignorant, not knowing the meaning of marriage, nor the resurrection, and then reminds them God is not the God of the dead, but of the living: "When the crowds heard this, they were astonished at his teaching" (Matthew 22:33). The crowds were astonished because His teaching was revolutionary. And that did not sit well with the so called experts.

For the Sadducees it seemed winning a debate was far more important than changing a life—even their own life. I still see the same attitude among many religious people today. You hear it when people say, "How can you claim to be a Christian and vote democratic?" You see it when people would rather quote propositional statements—"the Bible says . . ."—without first checking the accuracy of what the Bible really says. You see it when Christians would rather win an argument about abortion, homosexuality, capital punishment, or whatever—instead of trying to change the heart and life of other people, starting with themselves. Sometimes we are really quick to condemn *"phariseeism"* within the church when *"sadduceesim"* may be more prevalent and more dangerous. And while doctrine is important, Jesus' main purpose for coming into the world was not to create doctrine. His purpose was to proclaim the kingdom of God. His purpose was redemption—a changed life that brings about a changed world.

## ZEALOTS

As their name suggests, the Zealots were radicals. They saw themselves as "freedom fighters," defending the Law and Jewish nationalism against idolatrous Rome; and they were not opposed to using violence. The origin of the Zealots goes back to the Maccabean revolt. At least one disciple is known to have been part of this group—Simon the Zealot[19]; some believe Peter and Judas Iscariot were Zealots as well.

The problem with the Zealots was not their zeal, but their misplaced passion. Jesus admired their fervor; He simply tried to get them to focus on what was important. Passion is wonderful. Misplaced passion can be dangerous.

I don't remember exactly who it was, and it was probably more than one person, but over the years I have received the following advice: "Kevin, if you are going to survive ministry and make a difference in people's lives, you have got to decide on which battlefield you would be willing to die." At one time or another I think most people in ministry have had a tendency to fight the wrong battles. (I know I have.) When we have misplaced passion, and when we fight the wrong battles, the result is wounded soldiers who are serving the same God we are serving. "Friendly Fire" never defeats the enemy!

## ESSENES

Not much is known about the fourth group—the Essenes—mainly because they did not want much known about them. The Essenes were possibly a branch of the Pharisees, who considered the Pharisees too soft and liberal. The name itself means "pious," and in their piety they did not refer to themselves as *Essenes*, but was a name others gave them. Many Essenes lived in the desert (like hermits), but others lived in the cities and villages, mixing with society at all levels.

Strict obedience to the Torah was the primary feature of Essene behavior. They were known for their shared ownership of property, their hospitality to one another, and their disciplined life of prayer and study of the Old Testament. While stricter than the Pharisees, the Essenes carried far more respect among the people than the Pharisees or Sadducees. Their desire for piety came out of their sincere desire to follow and obey God. (Some biblical scholars speculate that John the Baptist was part of this sect. Other, more liberal scholars, speculate that Jesus was a member.)

People respected the Essenes, but they thought their lifestyles were strange, old- fashioned, and impractical. Apparently, in all their piety and disciplined lives, they did very little to change their world. The Essenes stayed in their own little groups, their own little "holy huddles."

We are probably more like the Essenes than we want to admit. After several recent conversations with non-believers, I have come to the following conclusion: *People may respect us, but they do not want to be like us.* Many unchurched people see the church as being outdated and irrelevant. They aren't nearly as impressed and enamored with our buildings, programs, and budgets as we are. I pray that as devout, disciplined followers of Jesus, we will strive to stay relevant in our culture, making a difference in our world.

When Jesus announced He was the Messiah, He did so in a culture where faithful Jews were waiting and looking for a political savior. At the same time, the Roman authorities were on the constant lookout for troublemakers within the Jewish community. Their goal was to keep the peace, keep themselves in power, and keep the Jews in submission.

The Pharisees, Sadducees, Zealots, and Essenes all had their idea of what the Messiah would do and be. Jesus did not fit any of their ideas—so they rejected Him. The Roman authorities really didn't see Jesus as a threat at all, and so they tried to ignore Him. The only reason they acted against Jesus was to keep peace with the Jewish religious leaders, especially their friends the Sadducees. Jesus thought outside the box, questioned the religious norms, and reached out to ordinary people. Some said He was an outlaw. God said, "You are my Son, whom I love; with you I am well pleased" (Mark 1:11).

## Rebel Yell

Christianity could use a few more troublemakers. Our culture needs a revolutionary. It is time for someone (maybe you) to stand up, be counted, and shake things up, not for self, but for Jesus! Complacency never got a person anywhere. Nice people never change the world. Nicer people get crucified by religious people.

This is not an excuse to cause trouble for the sake of causing trouble, but it is a challenge not to be afraid to be different. Don't be afraid to speak your mind. Don't be afraid to push the envelope. Don't be afraid to start a reformation. Remember, sometimes, *people, whom others consider to be a rebel, God considers to be a revolutionary.*

Are you a rebel or a revolutionary? Maybe a distinction between the two would be helpful. For sake of clarity, a rebel is someone who likes to cause trouble just for the sake of causing trouble. A rebel likes to push the buttons of authority figures, just for the reaction. A rebel picks fights for the enjoyment of fighting.

A revolutionary, on the other hand, is serving a cause greater than himself or herself. A revolutionary strives to change the world, making it a better place. From my perspective, a revolutionary is radically committed to following Jesus Christ. You can be a rebel without being revolutionary. But by its very nature, being a revolutionary means you are a rebel, at least every once in a while.

Do you desire to change your world? Your school? Your place of employment? Your church? Your family? Your life? Get ready; following Jesus was never meant to be easy, simple, or conventional. The journey following Jesus is a revolutionary journey filled with danger and adventure.

I dare you to be a revolutionary, to shake things up, to cause a little trouble. Again, not for the sake of being a troublemaker, but for the sake of being a radical follower of Jesus Christ. Before you accept this challenge, however, take a moment to stop and reflect. Are you headed in the right direction? Are you doing the right thing? Is your passion in the right place? Are your motivations pure? Are you willing to die on the right battlefield? Or, are you spinning your wheels? Are you wounding and being wounded in the wrong battle? Are you being different just for the sake of being different? Are you causing trouble just for the sake of causing trouble? Are you complacent? Lazy? Bored? Don't just stand up. Stand up for the right thing! Fight against the right enemy!

Nehemiah was a revolutionary. He stirred it up quite a bit by returning to his home land to rebuild a wall—both a physical wall and a symbolic wall. He met opposition. Some people tried to get him to quit, but he knew who his real enemy was. He said, "I am carrying on a great project and cannot go down. Why should the work stop?" (Nehemiah 6:3). He knew his opposition wasn't the real enemy. The real enemy was much more sinister. Likewise, "Our struggle is not against flesh and blood, but against the rulers, against the authorities, against the powers of this dark world and against the spiritual forces of evil in the heavenly realms" (Ephesians 6:12).

Shadrach, Mescach, and Abednego were revolutionaries. Even as prisoners in a strange land, they were not afraid to stand up for the One true God. They refused to compromise their values for expediency. They stood tall, and were willing to give their lives for their beliefs. Boldly, they proclaimed, "O Nebuchadnezzar, we do not need to defend ourselves before you in this matter. If we are thrown into the blazing furnace, the God we serve is able to save us from it, and he will rescue us from your hand, O king. But even if he does not, we want you to know, O king, that we will not serve your gods or worship the image of gold you have set up" (Daniel 3:16-18).

At one time, Saul was a rebel. He was more pious and more zealous about God than most others. He felt people

74

who were following "The Way" were dangerous to the religious establishment of the day. He arrested such people, and even participated in their stoning. But one day, on his way to arrest more Christians, Saul met Jesus (or rather, Jesus met Saul), and Saul the rebel, became Paul the revolutionary. And the rest is history.

After you take a moment to stop and reflect on what it means to be a revolutionary, pray for discernment. Praying for discernment is the only way you will be able to answer the previous questions. Being a revolutionary is not easy. Pioneers, explorers, and frontiersmen usually get shot . . . in the back. If you're going to cause trouble, make sure the trouble is because of the light you are shining in a dark place, not because you are personally offensive, arrogant, or sarcastic.

Speak the truth in love. People may shoot the messenger—just make sure it is the message they are mad at, not the messenger. Jesus proclaimed, "This is the verdict: Light has come into the world, but men loved darkness instead of light because their deeds were evil. Everyone who does evil hates the light, and will not come into the light for fear that his deeds will be exposed. But whoever lives by the truth comes into the light, so that it may be seen plainly that what he has done has been done through God" (John 3:19-21).

Another thing a rebel must do is count the cost. Jesus said, "Suppose one of you wants to build a tower. Will he not first sit down and estimate the cost to see if he has enough money to complete it? . . . Or suppose a king is about to go to war against another king. Will he not first sit down and consider whether he is able with ten thousand men to oppose the one coming against him with twenty thousand? . . . In the same way, any of you who does not give up everything he has cannot be my disciple" (Luke 14:28, 31, 33). This is why it is so important to stop, reflect, and pray for discernment. You've only got one life to live (and give), so make sure you live it to the fullest and give it for the highest cause. Doing so requires courage. Anyone can live for something, but only revolutionaries are willing to die for something bigger than themselves. The best way to spend your life is to be spent for the cause of Christ.

As a young boy he was different, some might call him eccentric. He graduated from high school at 14 and from college at 18. He studied engineering, but later answered the call to preach; and then later still, answered the call to missions as a medical missionary. He finished medical school at the top of his class. He could have gone anywhere to be a doctor, and he could have made a lot of money and done a lot of good. But after finishing medical school, he left the comforts of home (and a doctor's salary) to travel to the northeast corner of Ivory Coast, West Africa to serve the Lobi people of Doropo.

People thought he was crazy to take his young family so far away. But he wasn't crazy. Dr. LaVerne Miley was a modern day revolutionary. Today, the hospital he started in the "bush" country, still operates. Eight churches in the area owe their existence to his ministry.

Now it's your turn to walk courageously. Don't back down. Do what you know God has called you to do. Don't compromise. Jesus needs someone like you to change a world that desperately needs changing.

Never, ever, accept the status quo. Never, ever place religious rituals over real people . . . like the Pharisees.

Never, ever, place winning an argument above changing a life, even your own . . . like the Sadducees.

Never, ever, lose your passion. Just make sure it's not in the wrong place . . . like the Zealots.

Never, ever, be content to remain in your "holy huddle" . . . like the Essenes. Be a revolutionary. Shake things up. Cause a little bit of trouble for the sake of Christ.

---

## ENDNOTES

[1] This particular rumor gained popularity among Christianity's enemies in the second century as an attempt to discredit Jesus. The source of this rumor can be traced to Celsus, an anti-Christian philosopher whom

Origen (an early church father) quoted in his book, *Contra, Celsum.* Pantera—it is believed by critics of Christianity—was an archer in the Roman army.

[2]A book that was of great help to me for this section was *The Politics of Jesus,* written by Obery M. Hendricks Jr. (2006). While I did not agree with everything Hendricks said, I found a lot of his history to be insightful.

[3]Antiocus referred to himself as "Epiphanes," which means "God manifest."

[4]A pig was a detestable animal to the Israelites. Using it as a sacrifice was unimaginable.

[5]The reason I placed quotations around the word *free* is because the Israelites were still under Greek/Roman rule. They were no longer "oppressed," but they were not completely "liberated."

[6]597 B.C. is the approximate date of the Babylonian siege led by King Nebuchadnezzar.

[7]Cassius served under Marcus, was the brother-in-law of Brutus, and one of the major conspirators in the assassination of Julius Caesar.

[8]Flavious Josephus. *History of the Jewish War,* 1:342-346.

[9]Remember, biblical scholars place the birth of Jesus somewhere between 7 and 3 B.C.

[10]The Jewish historian, Josephus, mentions the revolt led by Judas the Galilean, writing, "Judas Galilean (and his followers) have a passion for liberty that is almost unquenchable, since they are convinced that God alone is their leader and master."

[11]It is easy to see the high regard the Jewish people felt for Mattathias and Judas by noting the number of people in the New Testament who were named either Matthew or Judas. In Jesus' day, both names were quite common.

[12]It is possible that Barabbas, whom the people asked to be released instead of Jesus, was such a troublemaker, as well as the two "robbers" crucified alongside Jesus. Thus, they were not common criminals, but, at least to some, they were "freedom fighters." This would explain why the local people were so quick to ask for Barabbas to be released instead of Jesus.

[13]By "religion" I mean the man-made aspects of our sacred practices, not those things which are part of Scripture. When those things, which are part of Scripture, lose their meaning and significance, it is our hearts and attitudes that must change, not the practice or discipline in Scripture. For example: The Lord's Supper is part of Scripture. When it loses its meaning, we are the problem, not the act itself.

[14]The reason this would be blasphemy was because only God can forgive sins. So either it was blasphemy or Jesus is God.

[15]The Sanhedrin was the Jewish supreme court.

[16]Matthew 26:66; 27:22-23.

[17]John 8:31-59.

[18]The entire encounter begins in verse 23 and goes through verse 40.

[19]Matthew 10:4; Mark 3:18; Luke 6:15.

## Questions for Discussion

1. How would you describe the cultural, political, and spiritual turmoil into which Jesus was born? Do you see any parallels between Jesus' day and our day? If so, what are those parallels?

2. Briefly describe the four different groups vying for the allegiance of the people in Jesus' day. How are each of these four groups seen in today's churches, among today's religious community?

3. How would you describe the difference between a rebel and a revolutionary when it comes to following Christ?

4. This chapter mentions the revolutionary examples of Jesus, Nehemiah, the three Hebrew children, and Paul, can you think of other examples of revolutionaries mentioned in Scripture? Can you think of modern day revolutionaries for Jesus Christ?

5. What could you do different this week, to be a revolutionary for the cause of Christ?

# 7 Was Jesus a Republican or Democrat?

"Once we get a handle on liberating the poor and oppressed, who are already alive, I will turn my attention to fighting for the rights of the unborn."

That was the answer my friend—an African American pastor—gave as to why he voted democratic in the last election. The person who asked the question was an upper-middle class, white, evangelical Christian, for whom the concept of any "God-fearing" person voting for a pro-choice party was unfathomable. The question was an honest inquiry into why the vast majority of African Americans consistently vote democratic.

I will admit at first I didn't like the answer. But the more I thought about it, the more it made sense. I'm still not sure I agree 100 percent, but his answer gives incredible insight to a perplexing question: *If Jesus were alive today, would He be a democrat or republican?* Closely related to this is the question: *Which political party best represents a Christian worldview?*

Some people consider the whole question of Jesus and politics to be a waste of time. After all, Jesus' mission was spiritual, not political. Thus, Jesus had nothing to say about politics and social issues. But that just isn't true! Jesus had plenty to say about social issues and social institutions. Yes, His primary mission was spiritual, but what He taught had tremendous social ramifications. Not to discuss Jesus' politics would be to leave out a significant portion of His life. Besides, Jesus came to redeem the world, and that includes the world of politics.

## The Kingdom of God

Jesus came preaching that the kingdom of God was a present reality, as well as a future hope.[1] The "kingdom of God" is an Old Testament idea, referring to a time when what God wills, "will be done on earth as it is in heaven" (Matthew 6:10). A key component of God's kingdom is justice and equality. Over and over again the prophets explained God's judgment as a result of how the Israelites mistreated and oppressed the weak of their society. Here is a sampling of the prophet's rebuke:

- *"'Take your evil deeds out of my sight! Stop doing wrong, learn to do right! Seek justice, encourage the oppressed. Defend the cause of the fatherless, plead the case of the widow. Come now, let us reason together,' says the LORD. 'Though your sins are like scarlet, they shall be as white as snow; though they are red as crimson, they shall be like wool'"* (Isaiah 1:16-18).

- *"For I know how many are your offenses and how great your sins. You oppress the righteous and take bribes and you deprive the poor of justice in the courts"* (Amos 5:12).

- *"But let justice roll on like a river, righteousness like a never-failing stream!"* (Amos 5:24).

- *"Woe to him who builds his palace by unrighteousness, his upper rooms by injustice, making his countrymen work for nothing, not paying them for their labor.... But your eyes and your heart are set only on dishonest gain, on shedding innocent blood and on oppression and extortion"* (Jeremiah 22:13, 17).

- *"And the word of the LORD came again to Zechariah: 'This is what the Lord Almighty says': "Administer true justice; show mercy and compassion to one another. Do not oppress the widow or the fatherless, the alien or the poor. In your hearts do not think evil of each other." But they refused to pay attention; stubbornly they turned their backs and stopped up their ears. They made their hearts as hard as flint and would not listen to the law or the words that the LORD Almighty had sent by his Spirit through earlier prophets. So the LORD Almighty was very angry. 'When I called, they did not listen; so when they called, I would not listen,' says the LORD Almighty."* (Zechariah 7:8-13).

After studying all these verses, plus many more, author Obery Hendricks concluded, "Prophetic speech is charac-terized by two elements: an overwhelming sense of an encounter with God and a message of moral and politi-cal judgment....The primary purpose of biblical prophecy is to effect social and political change in a society."[2] In fact, Hendricks believes two crite-ria can be used to identify a false prophet: (1) Silence about issues of social justice. (2) Uncritical supporters of people in governmental authority, instead of being the moral con-science of a society.[3]

> *Prophetic speech is characterized by two elements: an overwhelming sense of an encounter with God and a message of moral and political judgment .... The primary purpose of biblical prophecy is to effect social and political change in a society.*

What does all this have to do with Jesus?

EVERYTHING!

Jesus was the Prophet of all prophets. He made it clear He came, not to abolish the Law or the prophets, but to fulfill them completely.[4] On the day He announced His ministry in His hometown, He read the prophecy of Isaiah concerning the job description of the Messiah. The proph-ecy is from the opening verses of Isaiah 6. Jesus' words are in Luke 4:18-19: "The Spirit of the Lord is on me, because he has anointed me to preach good news to the poor. He has sent me to proclaim freedom for the prisoners and recovery of sight for the blind, to release the oppressed, to proclaim the year of the Lord's favor."

Provide programs to help the poor. Let prisoners out of prison after they have been rehabilitated. Provide health care. Spread freedom around the world. Sounds like a plat-form from which to launch a presidential campaign, doesn't it? Jesus' mission, though primarily spiritual, upset the social order of things. That, my friends, is a spiritual mission with tremen-dous political implications.

> *Jesus' mission, though primarily spiritual, upset the social order of things. That, my friends, is a spiritual mission with tremendous political implications.*

The New Testament writers understood this very well. The church in the book of Acts met together daily, assisting the poor and the oppressed: "All the believers were together and had everything in common. Selling their possessions and goods, they gave to anyone as he had need" (Acts 2:44-45). I don't know about you, but to me that sounds a lot like "redistribution of wealth." Along those same lines, Paul writes, "Command those who are rich in this present world not to be arrogant nor to put their hope in wealth, which is so uncertain, but to put their hope in God, who richly provides us with everything for our enjoyment. Command them to do good, to be rich in good deeds, and to be generous and willing to share" (1 Timothy 6:17-18). No one says it any clearer than James: "Religion that God our Father accepts as pure and faultless is this: to look after orphans and widows in their distress and to keep oneself from being polluted by the world" (James 1:27).[5] John writes, "If anyone has material possessions and sees his brother in need but has no pity on him, how can the love of God be in him?" (1 John 3:17).

Pastoral ministry has a way of hardening a person. For example, a young family in the church I was pastoring reached out to a single mom who was struggling financially. Because the holidays were coming, this family bought presents for the single mom's children. They also stocked her kitchen cabinets and refrigerator with groceries. All told, they spent several hundred dollars. A few days later they stopped by the mom's house and were horrified at what they saw. All the presents were gone, and there was nothing, absolutely nothing, in the kitchen cabinets and refrigerator. At first the mom claimed she had been robbed, but that was not the case. This single mom had sold and pawned everything she had been given so she could buy drugs!

The wife of the family in my church called me in tears. She vowed never to help anyone again. I know how she felt, and I knew she didn't really mean it. Her family is still generous with what they have, reaching out and helping others. I have seen this scenario happen over and over. At times it seems the majority of people who want help are nothing more than con artists. It's made me cynical. As a result, I have either ignored those needing help, or given assistance in order to get rid of them. Both approaches are wrong because neither show the love of Christ and advance the kingdom of God.

The gospel according to Jesus was the good news that God's kingdom was at hand; and that through faith in Him, you enter that kingdom. It was a present reality, as well as a future hope. After His resurrection, and before His ascension, Jesus met with His followers and told them not to "leave Jerusalem, but wait for the gift my Father promised" (Acts 1:4). The promised "gift" was empowerment by the Holy Spirit to continue the mission of Jesus, which was proclaiming and bringing about the kingdom of God.

His followers understood this, and so they asked Him, "Lord, are you at this time going to restore the kingdom of Israel?" (Acts 1:6).[6] Jesus informed them not to worry about the exact time of the fulfillment of God's kingdom, but to go and wait for the Holy Spirit. Once the Holy Spirit comes, then they will be able to continue bringing in the kingdom.

In Acts 2, the Holy Spirit filled all the disciples. Today, the Holy Spirit indwells each of us, enabling us to proclaim repentance, and advance God's kingdom in this world! And a huge component of that kingdom is preaching good news to the poor, proclaiming freedom for the prisoners and recovery of sight for the blind, releasing the oppressed.[7]

As a conservative, evangelical Christian, I am passionate about convincing people of their need to repeat the sinner's prayer. But how passionate am I about standing up for injustice, healing the sick, freeing the prisoners, and liberating the oppressed? How passionate am I about turning the social order on its head?

## The Sheep and the Goats

The parable of the sheep and goats is found in Matthew 25:31-46. This parable is the last in a series of parables about coming judgment. Jesus begins, "When the Son of Man comes in his glory, and all the angels with him, he will sit on his throne in heavenly glory. All the nations will be gathered before him, and he will separate the people one from another as a shepherd separates the sheep from the goats. He will put the sheep on his right and the goats on his left."[8]

Right away, you notice the symbolism of this story. Jesus is the "Son of Man," and on the day He comes in all His glory, the kingdom of God will be completely fulfilled. On this day—the culmination of God's kingdom—Jesus will separate people like a shepherd separates his sheep from his goats. Throughout Scripture, sheep symbolize the people of God; and goats, while not sinful in themselves, symbolize sin. In the Old Testament, a scapegoat was used to carry the sins of the people away from camp. So, in this story, Jesus places the sheep—His followers, people who believed in Him and continued His mission—on His right, a place of honor. On His left, a place of dishonor, He places the goats—people who rejected Him and His mission.

Now, if you are like me, you were taught that the way you became a "sheep" was by praying the sinner's prayer, confessing "Jesus is Lord." If you did so, on judgment day, you would go to your eternal reward. If you did not repeat that prayer, you would go to hell. I don't believe we were taught the wrong thing—salvation is by faith alone in Christ alone. I do, however, believe we have misunderstood what it means to be a follower of Jesus Christ.

Notice how Jesus explains the separation process:

"Then the King [Jesus] will say to those on his right [His sheep, His followers], 'Come, you who are blessed by my Father; take your inheritance, the kingdom prepared for you since the creation of the world. For I was hungry and you gave me something to eat, I was thirsty and you gave me something to drink, I was a stranger and you invited me in, I needed clothes and you clothed me, I was sick and you looked after me, I was in prison and you came to visit me"(Matthew 25:34-36).

Confused about the process, those on Jesus' right—the "righteous"—asked, "Lord, when did we see you hungry and feed you, or thirsty and give you something to drink?

When did we see you a stranger and invite you in, or needing clothes and clothe you? When did we see you sick or in prison and go to visit you?" (Matthew 25:37-39).

These are important questions because it reveals the righteous had been doing all these things regularly, and they had been doing them with the right motives. Doing these things was such a regular part of their life that they, at first, did not see the connection to doing these things for other people was the same as doing them for Jesus. They had been doing these things because they loved God and loved each other. They were not doing them expecting anything in return from anyone or anticipating that God was keeping score. They had fed the hungry, given something to drink to the thirsty, healed the sick, and liberated the oppressed, just as Jesus had modeled for them.

Jesus answered their questions, "I tell you the truth, whatever you did for one of the least of these brothers of mine,

> *Only in heaven will we see how much we owe to the poor for helping us to love God better because of them ... Each one of them is Jesus in disguise.*
> —Mother Teresa

you did for me" (Matthew 25:40).

Jesus then places the goats on His left, and repeats the entire speech. Except the goats did not feed the hungry, quench the thirsty, shelter the stranger, clothe the naked, nor care for the sick and imprisoned. Because they did not do those things, Jesus said, "Depart from me, you who are cursed, into the eternal fire prepared for the devil and his angels" (Matthew 25:41).

As a citizen of God's kingdom—which I become through faith in Jesus Christ—I am to be an ambassador of His kingdom, establishing kingdom satellites all around me, while I wait for Him to return. How do I establish kingdom satellites? By fighting for those who cannot fight for themselves. By speaking up for those who cannot speak for themselves. By taking care of those who cannot take care of themselves. By standing up for justice and equality, everywhere I see injustice and inequality; in politics, at work, at school, and even in the church. That's what it means to be a Christ-follower. That's what it means to be a citizen of the kingdom of God.

And here is the point: Spending your life standing up for one who cannot stand up for themselves is not a powerful, successful thing to do. Some people will look at you as a failure—"he had so much potential"—but doing so is exactly what it means to "fail like Jesus!" Success is not making a name for yourself, but making a name for the nameless and hopeless. That's the gospel in a nutshell.

## Challenging the System

It was this type of teaching and living that got Jesus in trouble with the authorities. It was this type of teaching and living that appeared to be one of His biggest failures. He constantly challenged the system. He continually stood up for the poor and oppressed.

On one occasion He violated the class (or caste) system of the day by talking to a Samaritan woman at a well.[9] The violation was three-pronged. First, He was a man talking to a woman (women had very little social standing in that day). Second, He was a Jew talking with a Samaritan. Samaritan's were considered "half-breeds," and were avoided by most Jews. Third, this woman was getting water, by herself, in the hot part of the day, meaning she was a woman who had a checkered history as an adulteress. Jesus upset the social order of the day by reaching out to her, extending an invitation to her to become part of the kingdom—an invitation she accepted.

On another occasion the Pharisees brought a woman to Jesus who had been caught in adultery. Intent on humiliating her and trapping Jesus, they stood the woman in the middle of the group and said to Jesus, "Teacher, this woman was caught in the act of adultery. In the Law Moses commanded us to stone such women. Now what do you say?" (John 8:4-5). The Law in question is found in both Leviticus 20:10 and Deuteronomy 22:22, which states that both the man and the woman caught in adultery should be stoned. So, one wonders, "where was the man with whom the woman committed adultery?" Furthermore, there is no evidence these Pharisees, or any other Jews in that era were carrying out this law in a literal way. (More than likely, the Romans would not have allowed it.) Thus, the sole purpose of this encounter was to humiliate the woman and trap Jesus.

Jesus did not take the bait. Instead, He "bent down and started to write on the ground with his finger" (John 8:6). Then I imagine that halfway through writing, as they continued questioning, Jesus stood back up and said, "If any one of you is without sin, let him be the first to throw a stone at her" (John 8:7). Jesus then stooped back down and continued writing. People have speculated what He wrote, but the Bible doesn't say. Apparently what He wrote, along with what He said, embarrassed the accusers, and so one by one they left until Jesus was alone with the adulteress.

"Jesus straightened up and asked her, 'Woman, where are they? Has no one condemned you?'

"No one, sir," she said.

'Then neither do I condemn you,' Jesus declared. 'Go now and leave your life of sin'" (John 8:10-11).

Jesus told another story possibly based on a real life experience.[10] In the story, a certain man was traveling from Jerusalem to Jericho. The man was robbed and left for dead on the side of the road. A priest came down the road, saw the injured man, and passed by on the other side, refusing to help. Next came a Levite. He also saw the injured man, but neither did he offer assistance. Instead, like the priest, he walked by on the other side of the road. The assumption was the victim was Jewish. The priest and the Levite, are not only Jews, they are also members of two different religious parties. Do you get the picture? A Jewish man lies dying in the street. Two, well respected Jews, ignore him.

Eventually a third man walks by. This third man was a Samaritan. To the audience Jesus was addressing, a Samaritan would have represented someone from the other side of the tracks. Someone not like the injured man at all. Maybe even someone of a different race or religion. This third man, the Samaritan, treated the guy's wounds, took him to a safe place, and paid for all his medical treatments.

Jesus' point was clear: *Loving people, meeting their needs when it is within your ability to do so, is the single most important thing you can do, regardless of your or their race, political affiliation, economic situation, or religious membership.*

When I was in college, one of the many jobs I had was as a "big brother" at a community center in Nashville, Tennessee. This organization served the poorest of the poor. I was a big brother to about 12 fourth graders. I would hang out with them for a few hours each day, and then take them home. They all lived in government housing in some of the worst areas of the city.

During my first stint as a pastor I lived and ministered in a very affluent community, one of the wealthiest in the entire country. During this time I still worked with organizations that helped the poor—feeding and clothing them, providing health care, etc. It was also during this time that I started teaching sociology at a community college. A big part of that class dealt with the issues of poverty, injustice, and inequality.

For 3.5 years I moved away from the affluent city to live and minister in another part of the country. During that time our home and church was in a poor part of town. One block away from our home was an apartment complex where some of the poorest people in the city lived. I learned a lot living in such a neighborhood.

Now I'm back living in an affluent city. But for some reason, I don't notice the affluence. I notice the poverty. I think I notice the poverty because of all the things God has allowed me to experience. God has opened my eyes. My perspective has changed. I believe being a follower of Jesus means standing up for the poor and oppressed, turning the social order of things upside down. Being the "light of the world" means we are to be the social conscience of our communities. Part of what it means to be a citizen of the kingdom of God means to bring that kingdom into reality in everyday life, while we wait for the fulfillment of that kingdom to come.

By siding with the oppressed, it seemed Jesus had failed. It is hard to change the power structure if you make enemies of those in power. But Jesus was not trying to set up a new, earthly political rule, He was very much interested in proclaiming the kingdom of God, and showing us glimpses of what that kingdom looks like.

I don't know about you, but I know if I am not careful I can become so consumed in providing my own needs that I forget about the needs of others. I can become so consumed in getting my own rights that I forget to stand up for the rights of others. We define success by how much we have, when we should be defining success by how much we give. A good verse for all of us to memorize, and put into practice, is Micah 6:8, "He has showed you, O man, what is good. And what does the Lord require of you? To act justly and to love mercy and to walk humbly with your God."

Jesus was neither a republican nor a democrat. He was, and is, the Lamb of God who takes away the sins of the world (John 1:29).

# ENDNOTES

[1]Matthew 4:17; Mark 1:15; and others.

[2]Obery M. Hendricks. 2006. *The Politics of Jesus.* New York: Doubleday Publishers (28). I can hear the objections now: "No! The primary purpose of the prophets was spiritual change and repentance." And that's the point I am trying to make. *You cannot separate spiritual change from moral and political implications!* What does this have to do with failing like Jesus? Well, politically speaking (just like spiritually speaking) it seemed Jesus failed. Once he died, and even after the resurrection, the political system did not change. The same people in power before where still in power after. However, everything had changed, and over time, those changes affected the entire world. Wherever Christianity has been introduced in the world, over time, the living conditions and aspects of justice have increased.

[3]Hendricks (31).

[4]Matthew 5:17.

[5]Orphans and widows are the most vulnerable people in any society. If James were writing today, he might possibly add "single moms" to the list. Single moms, their children, and widows make up a significant portion of people in our society who live below the poverty level.

[6]Saying, "kingdom of Israel" is another way of saying "kingdom of God."

[7]Adapted from Luke 4:18.

[8]Matthew 25:31-33.

[9]John 4:1-26.

[10]The story in mind is the Good Samaritan found in Luke 10:25-37.

# Questions for Discussion

1. Do you think it is important to discuss the political ramifications of Jesus' life and ministry? Why or why not?

2. What do you do, how do you react, when you feel like someone has taken advantage of your generosity? How do you keep from becoming cynical when such things take place?

3. Why is it important that Christians stand up for those who cannot stand up for themselves and speak out for those who cannot speak out for themselves?

4. Discuss the implications of Jesus' parable about sheep and goats.

5. What are the implications of living out Micah 6:8? How can you live this verse out this week?

# 8 A Reputation for Discarding His Reputation

Frank was a friend of mine, and an associate pastor at a large church in the city where I ministered. Frank grew up in (or near) that city. Me, I was the new guy. During my first week at my new assignment, while eating lunch at McDonalds with the pastoral staff of my church, in walked a man dressed like a woman. Those eating lunch with me said his name was Tim. Tim was the town's cross-dresser, and it was a small town in the buckle of the Bible belt.

In a small town, Tim was highly visible. Everyone knew about him, but very few knew his name. Tim walked everywhere he went, and so, almost daily, I would see him. He always dressed like a lady, always carried a purse, and he always wore make-up.

One Sunday, Tim visited Frank's church. Frank admitted that when he saw Tim in the hallway, his first thought was, "What is he doing here? I hope he doesn't disrupt things."

Frank walked past Tim without saying a word, hardly making eye contact. A few steps past Tim, according to Frank, God spoke directly to him saying in an almost audible voice, "You hypocrite! How can you say you love Me, and walk right past Tim?"

Frank, ashamed and embarrassed, turned around, walked up to Tim, introduced himself, and told him to let him know if he needed anything.

Tim kept attending church and over time starting dropping in to Frank's office during the week. Frank and Tim became friends. Sometimes they would eat lunch together at McDonalds. Frank's church, instead of judging Tim, embraced him and loved him. As Frank gained Tim's trust, Tim shared his story.

Tim's mother wanted a baby girl. When Tim was born, his mom immediately started dressing him in girl's clothes, and for all practical purposes, raised him as a daughter. Tim was smart. He had a master's degree in U.S. history and was certified to teach high school, but he could never hold a job. At a young age, to deal with the emotional confusion about his sexuality, Tim developed a split personality. Tim was his real name, the name on his birth certificate. Susan was his girl's name, and he had been living as Susan for years. In fact, on the Sunday Frank introduced himself to Tim, Tim referred to himself as Susan and wanted to be called Susan. However, in love, Frank told Tim he would never refer to him as Susan but always as Tim. Months into their relationship, Tim placed his faith in Jesus Christ, and vowed to never wear women's clothes again. (Before I knew the whole story, I remember noticing when I saw Tim around town that he had started wearing men's clothes.) Frank baptized Tim, while the church gave him a standing ovation.

Frank and I were part of a group of pastors that met weekly for coffee and conversation. One week, we talked in detail about Tim, and how Frank and his church had reached out to him. I wondered, as well as the other pastors, if my church would have embraced Tim as openly. I also wondered if I would have risked my reputation to befriend Tim. I had my doubts. We asked Frank if at any time he was worried about what others around town would think if they saw him and Tim together. He admitted the concern had crossed his mind, but God had spoken to him so clearly on that Sunday morning he knew he had no choice but to obey.

Don't you wish God would speak to you that clearly?

He has!

Jesus said, "If any one of you is without sin, let him be the first to throw a stone" (John 8:7).

That's pretty clear, don't you think?

## Reputation and Riff-Raff

If there was anyone who could have thrown stones, it was Jesus. After all, He was without sin. Yet He did not! Instead, He reached out to those no one else would.

What does it mean to "reach out"? That's a church phrase, but I wander if churches really know what it means. Typically, in church, the phrase "reach out" is used to discuss some type of event the church is going to sponsor in an attempt to get "new" people to attend. And so we "reach out" . . . usually to people just like us.

Every once in a while, feeling a little brave, we reach out to people who are different from us—socially, racially, economically, spiritually, etc. Thus, "outreach" events are usually a one time event at Christmas, Easter, or a block-party in the summer. Then we are back to our regular schedule, hanging around people just like us. We reach out and then keep people at arms' length . . . until the next outreach event.

As I think about the life of Jesus, and how He reached out to those who were different from the religious establishment of the day, I

> *As I think about the life of Jesus, and how He reached out to those who were different from the religious establishment of the day, I can't help but conclude that you have not really "reached out" to anyone unless you are willing to put your reputation on the line.*

can't help but conclude that you have not really "reached out" to anyone unless you are willing to put your reputation on the line.

Jesus was accused by the religious leaders of hanging out with the wrong crowd. He hung around people who could damage His reputation. But that didn't matter to Him because He wasn't a *separatist*. He wasn't afraid to hang out with the local riff-raff. He wasn't afraid to be seen with prostitutes, drunks. I even imagine He would not have been afraid to eat lunch with a cross-dressers at McDonalds. One of His own disciples, Matthew (or Levi), was such a person that others did not want to befriend.

Matthew was a Galilean born near the city of Capernaum. His parents, Alphaeus and Mary, were devout Jews. Matthew was brought up in a religious home. It must have broken his parent's heart when he decided to be a tax collector.

In the New Testament world being a tax collector was

the lowest of the low. The Jews considered the profession to be on the same level as prostitutes. Any Jew who became a tax collector (like Matthew) was considered a traitor. As a tax collector Matthew was a religious outcast, forbidden to enter the synagogue. The Jewish Talmud taught it was righteous to lie and deceive a tax collector because that was what a professional extortioner deserved. Roman taxation was handled by wealthy businessmen who paid a set fee for a contract to collect taxes in a specific area. Matthew must have been rich in order to buy his contract; and the only reason anyone would want such a contract was to become even wealthier. The tax collecting system was ripe for abuse. Every tax collector was assigned a certain amount of money to collect. Any overage was his to keep, and there was no oversight to protect the populace from whatever tax the tax collector wanted to charge. Tax collectors strong-armed money out of people with the use of thugs. A tax collector could make as much money as he could extract from the people, completely protected by the government.

Such was the profession of Matthew; a strong-armed, Mafia-type person with whom no God-fearing person would associate.

Jesus, not only associated with Matthew, He called him to be one of His closest followers—and He hung out with Matthew's friends. Here's how the story goes: "As Jesus went on from there, he saw a man named Matthew sitting at the tax collector's booth" (Matthew 9:9).

Jesus had been in His hometown. While there He healed a paralytic and had a brief confrontation with "some of the teachers of the law" (Matthew 9:3). After leaving, Jesus finds Matthew at his "tax collector's booth." More than likely, Matthew's tollbooth was located on the northern end of the Sea of Galilee, near the Syrian border, strategically located on a heavily traveled trade route from Damascus. One of the things Matthew taxed was fish caught in the Sea of Galilee. When Jesus saw Matthew, He said, "Follow me." Immediately "Matthew got up and followed Him" (Matthew 9:9).

Growing up in a devout Jewish home, Matthew learned the prophecies of the Old Testament. From his tax booth he heard the stories about Jesus and possibly witnessed a few of His miracles. Jesus knew Matthew was asking questions, seeking meaning and purpose in life. He knew Matthew was ready, and so when He challenged him, Matthew accepted without hesitation. Once Matthew "got up" he never again returned to his former profession.

What Matthew did was host a banquet for his friends, with Jesus as the guest of honor.[1] Since he was an outcast from the Jewish community, the only friends Matthew had were other "tax collectors and sinners" (Matthew 9:10). The word *sinners* could refer to anything from non-Jews, non-Pharisaical Jews, drunks, prostitutes, or people who were far from God. Chances are, at Matthew's party, all of the above type of "sinners" were present.

Matthew described this event by saying, "many . . . came and ate with him and his disciples" (Matthew 9:10). How many is "many?" No one knows for sure, but archaeologists have discovered homes from the New Testament world that could easily seat up to 500 people, just in the garden room. It is possible that hundreds attended this banquet. And all of them were seen as riff-raff by the religious community.

Jesus, eating with tax collectors and sinners, infuriated the Pharisees. Just eating with them indicated He included them in His fellowship, He considered them friends, and He approved of their lifestyles. Jesus responded, "It is not the healthy who need a doctor, but the sick. But go and learn what this means: 'I desire mercy, not sacrifice.' For I have not come to call the righteous, but sinners" (Matthew 9:12-13).

Considering Jesus was talking to people who thought they were experts on Scripture, the phrase "go and learn" was a stinging indictment. In essence, He was saying they did not know what they were talking about. What Jesus wanted them to relearn were the words spoken by God to the prophet Hosea, "I desire mercy, not sacrifice" (Hosea 6:6).

Offering sacrifices was fundamental to the Jewish faith in the Old Testament. Without sacrifices there was no forgiveness of sins. Jesus, being criticized for hanging around the wrong people, reminds the religious authorities that God prefers we show mercy to people over making sacrifices to Him. If Jesus were speaking today He might say, "I require mercy, more than I require church attendance." "I require you show people compassion, more than I require giving your money." It's not that our religious rituals are unimportant. After all, the New Testament clearly teaches us to worship together and give offerings. The heart of what Jesus said is that outward religious rituals mean nothing if you are more concerned with your reputation than you are meeting the needs of those around you.

Jesus' mission (and our mission) was not to stay in little clusters where He felt comfortable. After all, healthy people don't need a doctor. Jesus' mission (and our mission) was not to sit in His synagogue and say, "Come here if you need Me," but to go to where "sinners" are, calling them to a relationship with God. Jesus was criticized for hanging around the wrong people, but He criticized the religious for only hanging around the "right" people all the time. Outreach is not a program where you periodically invite people to a religious service. Outreach ("reaching out") is making a decision to live your life, building relationships with people far from God. Outreach is being willing to befriend those who need Jesus more than we need to maintain the façade of a good reputation.

## Building Relationships

How do you build relationships with people far from God? First and foremost you have to go where they are! You have to get out of your comfort zone, walk across your backyard, or across your office building lunchroom, and befriend someone who may not be like you. In order to gain the courage to do that you have to get over yourself and quit worrying about what other people are going to think. Yes, you will be criticized, but is that really enough to keep you from following God?

For several years now I have been involved with a group

of Christian men whose main mission is to seek reconciliation across racial, denominational, and economical lines.
My life has been deeply enriched by my interactions with
these individuals who come from all different walks of life.
One of the key things I have learned from them is the idea
of *intentionality*. Reaching out, beyond our comfort zones,
does not come easily for most of us. I have to be intentional
about it. I have to want to. I have to put myself in situations
where I have the opportunity to reach out to people who
are different from me. Intentionality takes time and it takes
sacrifice. Sometimes people will misunderstand, or misin-
terpret, what you are doing.

In order to reach out, you must get beyond relationships
of convenience (*transactional relationships*), to relationships
of purpose (*transformational relationships*). Relationships of
convenience are easy, practical, and comfortable. Convenient
relationships are with people who are just like you—socially,
racially, politically, economically, religiously, etc. You build
these types of relationships for what you can give and get
out of them. There's an exchange that takes place. You put
something into them and expect something out of them.
Relationships of convenience are not bad. In fact, we need
these in our life. We just need more.

God has called us to something more. Something deeper. Something life-changing. Something transformational.
Transformational relationships mean that people are different—for the good—because of your interactions with them.
Building these types of relationships changes the other person and me; the changes make us both better people. These
types of relationships are inconvenient and difficult, but they
are priceless. I am to reach out to others, not to meet a need,
and not to get something in return (that's *transactional*). I
am to reach out because God wants to transform me into
the image of Christ, and He wants to use me as an instru-
ment of transformation in other people's lives. What are we
changing, and who are we changing, if we only reach out to
people who are already like us?

## Throw a Party

On another occasion Jesus was invited to dinner in the home of a prominent Pharisee.[2] He knew while He was at this house He would be carefully watched. At the dinner He noticed how people tried to choose "places of honor" around the table. Who was going to sit at the head of the table? How can I get a seat close to the front?

Isn't it interesting how people always try to network and position themselves in order to better themselves? Those at the dinner were building *transactional relationships*.

According to Jesus, we should be willing to be the runt of the pack instead of fighting to be the top dog. It wasn't about networking and net worth, but about humility and service. He says, "For everyone who exalts himself will be humbled, and he who humbles himself will be exalted" (Luke 14:11).

Jesus continues His discourse with a startling statement: "When you give a luncheon or dinner, do not invite your friends, your brothers or relatives, or your rich neighbors; if you do, they may invite you back and so you will be repaid" (Luke 14:12).

In other words, don't just build transactional, convenient relationships!

Instead, when throwing a party, "invite the poor, the crippled, the lame, the blind, and you will be blessed. Although they cannot repay you, you will be repaid at the resurrection of the righteous" (Luke 14:13-14).

In other words, build transformational, inconvenient and purposeful relationships!

To further explain His point, Jesus told a story. In the story a man throws a lavish party. He sent invitations to all his friends, neighbors, co-workers, and family. He then followed up the invitations by sending his personal servants to pick up the guests and bring them to the banquet.

Surprisingly, all the invited guest made excuses for why they could not attend: "I have just bought a field, and I must go and see it . . . . I have just bought five yoke of oxen, and I'm on my way to try them out . . . . I just got married" (Luke 14:18-20).

When the servants reported the news, the host was furious! *How could they do this to me? I have prepared all this food and everyone is standing me up?*

Undeterred, the man ordered his servants to go into the "streets and alleys . . . and bring in the poor, the crippled, the blind and the lame" (Luke 14:21).

After the servants had done what the host told them, they came back and reported, "Sir . . . what you ordered has been done, but there is still room" (Luke 14:22). And so the man said, "Go out to the roads and country lanes and make them come in, so that my house will be full" (Luke 14:23). And so the servants went out and gathered the homeless and brought them in.

Through this story, Jesus was saying that God is getting ready to throw a party. In Jesus Christ the invitations have gone out, but those who you thought would come—the religious—have all made excuses, and so they will miss the party completely.[3]

Instead of being rejected, God's invitation goes out to those who most need it—those who are hurting physically, emotionally, and spiritually. Likewise, you and I gain nothing if we keep trying to reach out to people who are comfortable or who continually make excuses . . . people like ourselves. Our mission is to invite the poor, the hurting, the homeless, those everyone else has rejected, and invite them to the greatest party ever thrown. We will not, and cannot, fulfill our mission by only entertaining people who act like us, dress like us, smell like us, and look like us.

Another example is seen in Jesus' encounter with a man named Zacchaeus.

Like Matthew, Zacchaeus was a tax collector, meaning he had more enemies than friends. But he wasn't just any run of the mill tax collector; "he was a chief tax collector and was wealthy" (Luke 19:2). He wasn't just a crook; he was the leader in a gang of crooks. Socially speaking, Zacchaeus was the worst of the worst, while at the same time the wealthiest of the wealthy.

Being the "height-challenged" man that he was, Zacchaeus climbed a tree to see over the crowds for a glimpse of Jesus.

As surprising as it was that a man like him would be looking for Jesus, it is also surprising Jesus was looking for a man like him. In a very bold move, when Jesus saw Zacchaeus, He invited Himself to his house. It would be one thing for a person of questionable character to invite you to his or her home; you could politely decline that invitation. But to invite yourself to a questionable person's home, that's unthinkable! The people could not believe Jesus was going to socialize with such a person. The people "muttered" (or grumbled) to themselves, "He has gone to be the guest of a 'sinner'" (Luke 19:7).

Once again, there goes Jesus' reputation.

But Jesus was about *transformation* not *transaction*, and so He saw something in Zacchaeus that no one else saw. Zacchaeus had been changed. Jesus said, "Today salvation has come to this house, because this man too, is a son of Abraham" (Luke 19:9).

> *Heaven and hell will be decided, not only on what you do with Jesus, but what you did with the poor, the sick, and the oppressed among you!*

And then, using Zacchaeus as an example, Jesus revealed His mission statement: "The Son of Man came to seek and to save what was lost" (Luke 19:10).

Jesus gave His life for the down and out, the despised and rejected, and the disenfranchised of society . . . just like you and I were . . . and He has called us to do the same.

"But doesn't bad company corrupt good character?" some might say. On the one hand, yes. But on the other hand, the only way those who truly need Jesus are ever going to hear about Jesus is if those of us who know Jesus build intentional, transformational, purposeful relationships with them. There really is no other way. Someone, maybe you and maybe me, must be willing to put our reputations on the line in order to reach out to those who need it most.

Are you willing?

Am I willing?

## ENDNOTES

1. Matthew 9:10-13.
2. Luke 14:1-24.
3. Luke 14:24.

# Questions for Discussion

1. What do you think about the opening story? How would you react, given the same situation? Do you think your church would have been accepting of Tim?

2. What do you think it means to "reach out"? Can you think of situations where reaching out put your reputation on the line?

3. What do you think Jesus meant when He said that it was the sick who needed a doctor, not the healthy? (Matthew 9:12-13)

4. Explain in your own words the difference between transactional relationships and transformational relationships. What are some examples of each in your life?

5. What are some things you can do to intentionally reach out and build relationships with people who are different from you?

# A Terrible Temper

Do you think God ever loses His cool? Does He ever get angry? Does He have a temper?

It's hard to picture Jesus angry. After all, Jesus is loving, kind, and compassionate. It's hard to imagine Him losing His temper.

There is a story found in all four gospels that tells of a time when Jesus seemed to have completely lost His cool.[1] It's a story that shows a side of Jesus that most pictures of Him don't show. And while we know that His temper was completely justified, if you were a witness to it on that day, you would think He was going too far. The story also illustrates that in certain situations, it is perfectly acceptable to passionately speak your mind. Following Jesus doesn't mean you have to be timid and meek and mild. Just make sure when you do get angry (maybe passionate is a better word), it's for the right reasons. We usually get angry at the wrong things, at the wrong times and for the wrong reasons.

## Cursing the Fig Tree and Clearing the Temple

Mondays can be difficult, can't they? Mondays are a terrible way to spend one-seventh of your life. A lot of people hate Mondays.

Jesus' righteous temper manifested itself on a Monday.

In Mark 11, Mark describes events that took place during the week leading up to Jesus' crucifixion. During this week, Jesus and His disciples spent the evenings in the town of Bethany[2] and their days in the city of Jerusalem. Mark records, "The next day as they [Jesus and His disciples] were leaving Bethany . . . ." (Mark 11:12). The "next day" was the day after Jesus' parade into Jerusalem—the day we now call "Palm Sunday,"[3] the beginning of Holy Week (or Passion Week); and so, the "next day" was Monday. Jesus knows how this week is going to end, and so I imagine He was under a tremendous amount of stress, and maybe just a little on edge.

Jesus never sinned, but that doesn't mean He did not feel the pressures and stresses of life like we do. After all, He was human.

On Monday morning, as Jesus and His disciples walked the two miles from Bethany to Jerusalem, something very human happens to Jesus; He gets hungry: "Seeing in the distance a fig tree in leaf, he went to find out if it had any fruit. When he reached it, he found nothing but leaves, because it was not the season for figs. Then he said to the tree, 'May no one ever eat fruit from you again.' And his disciples heard him say it." (Mark 11:113-14).

What just happened, and what does it mean? Why does Jesus condemn a fruitless tree that wasn't in season to have fruit?

Jesus' cursing the fig tree is the last miracle (except for the resurrection) in Mark's gospel, and it is the only miracle Jesus performed that destroyed life instead of giving life. What was Jesus trying to communicate in His seemingly harsh words?

Mark returns to the fig tree in 11:20, but sandwiched in between the two events with the fig tree is another account of Jesus seemingly getting angry. It's still Monday, but this time He clears out the temple area.[4] The cleansing of the temple within the story of the cursing of the fig tree means the two stories help interpret each other, giving insight into the intended message.

The best explanation of cursing the fig tree and cleansing the temple is that Jesus was illustrating a parable about the coming judgment of Jerusalem. Old Testament prophets frequently spoke of the fig tree in reference to Israel's status before God. When Jesus saw the fig tree from a distance, it had foliage on it. Although it wasn't the normal time of year for there to be fruit, this tree had the appearance of fruit, but upon closer examination, it was barren.[5] Jesus curses the tree for its hypocrisy—appearing to be one thing while in reality being something else.

While Jesus is kind and compassionate, there is another side to Him. There are some things that make Him righteously angry, and hypocrisy is one of those things. *Hypocrisy is not being and doing what you were created to be and do . . . just like the fig tree.*

The fig tree was created to be fruitful, providing nourishment for others. Outwardly the tree looked like it was being and doing what it was created to be and do, but inwardly it was empty.

Likewise, Jesus created you for a purpose. He created you to have a relationship with Him. He made you unique, giving you specific talents and gifts. There is a reason you were put on this planet. It is only through a personal relationship with Jesus Christ that you will ever fulfill your purpose and reach your full, God-given potential. Without Him, life is meaningless and empty. There is a *loss of purpose* when you are not doing and being what you were created to do and be.

Mark continues, "On reaching Jerusalem, Jesus entered the temple area and began driving out those who were buying and selling there. He overturned the tables of the money changers and the benches of those selling doves, and would not allow anyone to carry merchandise through the temple courts. And as he taught them, he said, 'Is it not written: My house will be called a house of prayer for all nations'? But you have made it a 'den of robbers?'" (Mark 11:15-17).[6]

Why the strong reaction?

The previous evening Jesus went to the temple and looked around, but apparently the "market area" had closed for the day.[7] Now He returns, and He is on a mission because He knows time is running out, His earthly ministry was quickly coming to an end. Like the fig tree, the present condition of Judaism was one of hypocrisy, and that hypocrisy was mostly seen in the activities surrounding the temple. The "temple area," where Jesus goes into His righteous rage, was in the Court of the Gentiles.

Tens of thousands of people where lingering in and out of the temple area, celebrating the Passover, purchasing animals and incense and jewelry, and other items to be used in the religious ceremonies of the week—such as wine, oil, and salt—all required by the Old Testament Law. The Court of the Gentiles had turned into a flea market and cattle mart. Religion had become big business. It was all taking place in the only area a non-Jew could worship God!

This commercialization was totally unnecessary. Outside the temple area, on the Mount of Olives, were approved markets for the same purpose. However, the priests did not get a cut of everything sold outside the temple area. Inside, they made a lot of money. Thus the priests opened up the temple area to line their own pockets.

More deplorable than the merchants were the "money changers." Once a year all Jews were required to pay a temple tax. The common coin was the Roman coin, but the Roman coin was unacceptable for the temple tax. Thus, the Roman coin had to be exchanged for a Hebrew coin, and the exchange rate being charged was astronomical. This brings up another thing that makes Jesus angry. *Jesus gets angry when we don't take worship seriously.* Jesus gets angry, rightfully so, when religion becomes big business. The result of not taking worship seriously is a loss of *power.*

Mark now returns to the fig tree, "In the morning, as they went along, they saw the fig tree withered from the roots" (Mark 11:20-21). It is now Tuesday, and as Jesus walks back to Jerusalem, His disciples notice that the tree Jesus cursed has withered. Mark continues, "They arrived again in Jerusalem, and while Jesus was walking in the temple courts, the chief priests, the teachers of the law and the elders came to him. 'By what authority are you doing these things?' they asked. 'And who gave you authority to do this?'" (Mark 11:27-28).

There is no doubt the religious leaders were still upset about what they thought was an emotional outburst on the previous day. *Who did Jesus think He was?*

Jesus asked the religious leaders a question they could not answer. So in response, He said, "Neither will I tell you by what authority I am doing these things" (Mark 11:33). Jesus wasn't being rude, and He wasn't running out of patience. He was simply being poignant. He was tired of playing their games. They were asking questions that they didn't really want answered. Likewise today, Jesus doesn't like it when people ask questions, but don't want answers. Jesus doesn't like it when people don't honestly seek Him.

God doesn't mind your questions, your doubts, and your concerns. All He asks is that you honestly seek Him, and open yourself up to Him. He will prove Himself real in your life. But if all you are doing is looking for reasons not to believe, looking for something else to criticize, looking for another way to undermine His authority, well, God may not answer you, and without answers it is really difficult to know what to do. The result of not honestly seeking Him is a *loss of potential.*

## Lifting the Curse, Making Things Right

On Tuesday morning, when Jesus and His disciples were going back to Jerusalem, they came to the fig tree Jesus had cursed. Peter makes reference to it, and Jesus says, "Have faith in God . . . . I tell you the truth, if anyone says to this mountain, 'Go, throw yourself into the sea,' and does not doubt in his heart but believes that what he says will happen, it will be done for him. Therefore I tell you, whatever you ask for in prayer, believe that you have received it, and it will be yours. And when you stand praying, if you hold anything against anyone, forgive him, so that your Father in heaven may forgive you your sins"(Mark 11:22-26).

Nowhere does Jesus explain why He did what He did. However, if the cursing of the fig tree and cleansing the temple had to do with the coming judgment on Israel because of her hypocrisy, then His response to Peter must be how to avoid the coming judgment. Jesus was telling His disciples, and us, how not to wind up like the fig tree and temple merchants.

How do I avoid the fate of the fig tree? First, by having faith. Don't just believe in anything, believe in Jesus. Don't place your faith in your ability, but in the ability of Jesus. Don't place your faith in faith; rather, "have faith in God." Have unwavering faith in Him. Commit your entire life to Him, and He will restore your *purpose.*

The second thing you must do is pray. And have faith when you pray. Anything that runs on electricity must be plugged into the electricity to receive any power. Likewise, the Christian life runs on the power of prayer. However, you must stay plugged into the power to receive any power. Prayer will regain your *power*.

Next, Jesus tells us the most difficult thing to do, and that is to forgive. Jesus made it clear that if you don't forgive others, He will not forgive you. There is no room in a believer's life for bitterness and resentment. It is through forgiveness that you will regain your *potential*.

When you were a child, did your parents ever discipline you while saying, "This hurts me more than it hurts you"? Did you believe them? Now, as a parent, have you ever disciplined your child and it broke your heart? Do you now understand what your parents were saying?

Why does it break a parent's heart when a child does something wrong? Because as parents we want more for our children than we want for ourselves. A parent understands their child's purpose, power, and potential. A parent gets upset, not because the child's wrong affects the parent, but because the parent knows the affect the wrong will have on the child. Likewise, Jesus doesn't get angry because what we have done—or not done—somehow affects Him, but because He loves us, and wants more for us than we want for ourselves; He knows how our wrongs affect us.

Today, right now, you can rediscover your purpose through faith; restore your power through prayer; and release your potential through forgiveness. Let Jesus cleanse the temple of your heart, lift the curse from your fruitless life, and restore you to Himself.

# ENDNOTES

[1] The story of Jesus losing His temper can be found in Matthew 21:12-13; Mark 11:15-17; Luke 19:45-46; and John 2:12-16. I will look mainly at Mark's account because he places it in the context of Jesus cursing a fig tree as well.

[2] Bethany was a small village on the southeastern slopes of the Mount of Olives, approximately 2 miles east of Jerusalem. Bethany was the hometown of Mary, Martha, and Lazarus. Jesus and His disciples probably stayed in their home during the week. It is quite possible that the reason Jesus stayed out of Jerusalem at night was because of threats to His life by the religious leaders in Jerusalem.

[3] Mark 11:1-11.

[4] Mark 11:15-19.

[5] Fig trees in Jerusalem usually leaf out in March or April, but do not produce figs until June. This places this event in the spring, during the time of Passover. Early green figs, which actually appear before the leaves, could be expected at this time, and though they are disagreeable in taste, they can be eaten.

[6] The quotes in v. 17 are from Isaiah 56:7 and Jeremiah 7:11.

[7] Mark 11:11.

# Questions for Discussion

1. People don't like to think about Jesus getting angry. Why do you think that is? Is anger, in and of itself a sin?

2. Why does Jesus condemn the fig tree? Why does Jesus overturn the tables at the temple?

3. Three things were mentioned in this chapter as causing Jesus to become righteously angry. What were those three things? What is the result of those three things? Which one of the three stood out most to you? Why?

4. According to Jesus, what three things need to be done so that we don't receive the same curse the fig tree received? Of those three, which one do you think is the most important? Why?

# 10

# This Is Not What
# I Signed Up For

Abandoned by his Danish father before he was born, teased at a Jewish school because he was German, only to later be teased at a grammar school because he was Jewish, Erik Erickson understood the unfairness of life.[1] Later in his life, when the Nazis took control of Germany, Erickson fled first to Denmark and then to the United States. Erickson used his experiences of rejection and fear to become one of the most influential psychologists of modern time. His greatest contribution to the field of psychology was his belief that personality is shaped throughout a person's entire life as they pass through eight stages.[2] Each stage, Erikson believed, is marked by conflict around a key event, and how we handle that conflict prepares us for the next stage.

Right now I am passing through the Middle Adulthood stage where the main event is parenting. According to Erickson, the conflict at this stage is between making a difference in the world or becoming self-absorbed. Some people call this stage a mid-life crisis. Here is how it works:

In your twenties you are full of dreams of what you are going to do and what you are going to become. You live in a world of ideals and you have plenty of ideas about the world. The twenties are great fun. The problem is they are followed by the thirties. During our thirties our idealism turns into realism. In extreme cases idealism turns into fatalism. And then comes the forties.

Somewhere around the age of 40 it dawns on people, *I am running out of time. My life is half over and what have I accomplished?* For some people the answer to this question involves buying a new sports car or trading in the old spouse for a newer, younger one. For others, switching careers is the answer. (All are forms of self-absorption.) According to Erikson, however, the healthy response at this stage is to pour your life into the next generation, leaving them a legacy. That's how you make a difference.

And then comes the final stage, Old Age, beginning around the age of 65, according to Erikson. How you handle the conflict at each stage prepares you for the next stage. If during the previous stage (Middle Adulthood) you were self-absorbed, then at this final stage of life you will experience despair. On the other hand, at this stage in your life as you look back over your life, if you have developed properly, and if you have tried to make a difference, then during Old Age you will experience integrity—a sense that you have lived a full, meaningful life. You will conclude that through all the ups and downs and good and bad of life, life was worth it; and you would want to do it all over again if you could.

All of life, at every stage, is full of ups and downs, good and bad, isn't it? During the good times it seems that life is worth it, but during the bad times we wonder if it will ever get better. Will it be worth it? Right now, if life is good, great! But I want to talk to those who may be struggling. I want to address those who may be on the verge of throwing up their hands screaming, "What's the point! What's the use!" I want to talk to those who are battling the monster called "life ain't turned out like I thought it would." If you are in that situation, here is what I want to say:

Don't give up! Hang in there! What you are experiencing is something everyone experiences. And it can happen at any time, during any of the life stages Everyone has a moment of crisis in their life when they think, "God, this is unfair. Life was not supposed to work out this way. This is not what I signed up for."

Even Jesus struggled through this experience.

## Betrayal, Bread, and Blood

On the one hand, because He was God, Jesus knew His destiny was the cross. Redemption, grace, forgiveness, and mercy were all His ideas. It's what He signed up for. But on the other hand, because He was human, Jesus did not look forward to what He was going to endure. From an earthly perspective, near the end of His life, things were not looking good. If you were an outsider looking in on the events surrounding Jesus, you would conclude that He was a failure, things were not going as planned. This was not what He had signed up for. Jesus was entering His moment of crisis.

And it started with a betrayal.

Some words, in and of themselves, sound bad. Some words need no definition. Such is the word *betrayed*. There's a hint of the word *traitor* in it. There is no way to use the word *betrayed* or *betrayal* in a positive manner. For example, in certain contexts saying something is "bad" really means it is "good": *That new car of mine is one bad ride.* Sometimes a "bomb" is good: *That movie was the bomb.* In certain situations, even "killing" can be positive. A parent can ask his teenage son, "How did you do on your test today?" And the son will answer, "I killed it," meaning he did very well. But not so with the word *betrayal*. Regardless of the context, betrayal is always bad and it always hurts. Betrayal hurts because only those closest to you can really betray you. An enemy can't betray you. Only a friend can be guilty of such a crime.

> "So they counted out for him thirty silver coins" (Matthew 26:15): *The counting out of thirty silver coins calls to mind Zechariah 11:12. This amount was the price of a slave accidentally gored to death by an ox [Exodus 21:32]. The identity of the coin is not specified, but a manuscript variant [suggests the coin used was the most common coin used for paying the temple tax]. It was the equivalent of four denarii, so that amount is equivalent to four months' wages, or about $5,000.*
> —Taken from Zondervan Illustrated Bible Backgrounds Commentary; vol. 1 "Matthew, Mark, Luke," Clinton E. Arnold, General Editor (p. 162).

Matthew records, "Then one of the Twelve—the one called Judas Iscariot—went to the chief priests and asked, 'What are you willing to give me if I hand [Jesus] over to you?' So they counted out for him thirty silver coins. From then on Judas watched for an opportunity to hand him over" (Matthew 26:14-16).

And what better opportunity than after a meal!

For people, the event of being together, sharing a meal, is as important as the meal itself. And so the disciples asked Jesus, "Where do you want us to make preparations for you to eat the Passover?" (Matthew 26:27).

115

Jesus replied, "Go into the city to a certain man and tell him, 'The Teacher says: My appointed time is near. I am going to celebrate the Passover with my disciples at your house'" (Matthew 26:18).

Jesus tries to put a positive spin on the upcoming events. He wants it to be a happy occasion, even though He knows what the night holds. "When evening came, Jesus was reclining at the table with the Twelve. And while they were eating, He said, 'I tell you the truth, one of you will betray me'" (Matthew 26:21).

There's that word, *betray*. What an ugly word. The word means to be "handed over." It is one thing to be taken by force, or by surprise, but it is quite another thing to be quietly handed over to your enemies by your closest friend. You can't put up a fight when you have been betrayed. Betrayal breaks the heart and the will of the person.

Jesus knew Judas was going to betray Him. He even said as much at the dinner, but no one could imagine one of Jesus' closest followers turning on Him, especially Judas. Judas was a zealot. Judas was willing to fight to the death to protect Jesus. Matthew, a former low-life tax collector might betray Jesus, but not Judas.

The next thing to happen at this celebration dinner is utterly beyond human comprehension.

Matthew records, "While they were eating, Jesus took bread, gave thanks and broke it, and gave it to his disciples, saying, 'Take and eat; this is my body.' Then he took the cup, gave thanks and offered it to them, saying, 'Drink from it, all of you. This is my blood of the covenant, which is poured out for many for the forgiveness of sins'" (Matthew 26:26-28).

After announcing He was going to be betrayed, Jesus began the most holy and sacred event in all of Christendom. He gave each disciple, including Judas His betrayer, the bread and the cup which symbolized His broken body and spilled blood. In essence, Jesus forgave the betrayer before the betrayer betrayed! It's called grace, and it is amazing. And if Jesus was willing, and able, to forgive Judas, then He is willing, and able, to forgive you, regardless of what you have done.

Do you need His forgiveness? Do you feel far from God? Does God feel far from you? Like Judas, have you betrayed the One you love?

Whatever you have done really doesn't matter. Jesus has already forgiven you. All you have to do is accept His forgiveness. Accept it like you would a piece of bread—His body that was broken for you; and a cup of squeezed grapes—His blood that was poured out for you. His provision for your forgiveness is more than adequate for any wrong you may have committed.

To often we focus to much on Judas betrayal in this story instead of focusing on the amazing love, grace, mercy, and forgiveness of Jesus. Sadly, Judas did not accept Jesus' forgiveness and went forward with his betrayal.

## This Is Not What I Signed Up For

In Jesus' day, in the city of Jerusalem, there were very few, if any private or public gardens. However, the elite of that society did have gardens on the slopes of the Mount of Olives outside the city. One such unnamed person had given Jesus permission to use his garden any time He was in town; and apparently on several occasions Jesus had used this particular garden to go and pray. Judas knew this, and he knew exactly where Jesus would be. That is why he was in a position to hand Jesus over to the authorities without causing any trouble.

Jesus, along with His disciples went to this garden called Gethsemane. The word *Gethsemane* means "oil-press." Gethsemane was a garden of olive tree groves used to make olive oil.

Upon entering the garden, Jesus took Peter, James, and John deeper into the garden to pray. He said to the three of them, "My soul is overwhelmed with sorrow to the point of death. Stay here and keep watch with me" (Matthew 26:38).

Next, Matthew records, "Going a little farther, he fell with his face to the ground and prayed, 'My Father, if it is possible, may this cup be taken from me'" (Matthew 26:39).

Please read this next line carefully, and make sure you read the rest of this chapter so that you will not misunderstand what I am saying. Are you ready? You have been warned. Read the following words carefully: *Jesus did not want to die!*

Let that sink in.

*Jesus, the man, did not want to die!*

It was at this moment that Jesus, in His humanity, like you and I, faced the darkest moment of His life. In a sense He was saying, "Lord, does it really have to be this way? I am not sure I can do it. I am not sure this is what I signed up for. I am not sure if this is how My life was supposed to turn out. There's got to be an easier way. Life should not be this difficult."

Less than a week earlier, Jesus (the man) was on top of the world. Now He is at the bottom of the lowest valley possible. Luke, a medical doctor as well as a historian, in his record of the events at Gethsemane, explains, "And being in anguish, he prayed more earnestly, and his sweat was like drops of blood falling to the ground" (Luke 22:44). I am told there is a medical term for this condition. All I know is that while I have had health issues due to stress, I have never sweated drops of blood. The pressure of life was killing

Two primary sites for the actual location of Gethsemane have claimed scholar's attention. The first site now houses the Church of All Nations (or the Franciscan Basilica of the Agony), which is adjacent to an olive grove about fifty-five yards square, with olive trees perhaps more than a thousand years old. . . . The second site is perhaps more promising, which is located a few hundred feet north of the traditional garden, slightly lower on the Mount of Olives. The cave is quite large, measuring approximately 36 by 60 feet . . . with interior caves cut into the walls for locating oil presses. Some suggest that a cultivated garden area originally surrounded the cave within the olive groves on the hill. After an extensive archaeological reconstruction, one archaeologist suggests that the disciples went to the cultivated garden area to sleep in the cave that they had frequented on other occasions. Once there, Jesus asked the inner group of disciples to stay awake with Him while He prayed. The soldiers came to the garden area and found Jesus praying there, with the disciples asleep in the cave.
—Taken from *Zondervan Illustrated Bible Backgrounds Commentary;* v. 1, "Matthew, Mark, Luke" (p. 166).

Jesus, *but He did not want to die.*

A lesser man would not have been able to continue.

Jesus was a man's man. Somehow, and from somewhere deep inside, He found the strength to continue, and in so doing He prayed the most incredible prayer in the entire Bible. Jesus prayed, "Yet not as I will, but as you will" (Matthew 26:39). These nine short words changed the course of history.

Jesus did not want to die. What He did want, more than anything else, even more than life, was to do what God willed!

Where did Jesus, the man, get the courage, strength, and confidence to completely submit Himself to God's plan for His life?

I believe His courage, strength, and confidence came from trusting in God's sovereignty. Jesus, the man, was saying, "God, this may not be the plan I would create for My life, but I trust in Your plan. You know what You are doing. You know what is best."

Right now, your life may not look like it has had a plan. Right now

In the Bible the metaphor of a "cup" could be positive or negative. A "cup" could represent life, nourishment, and fellowship. It can also represent a curse, drunkenness, and death. The psalmist said, "my cup overflows" (Psalm 23:5). However, God's judgment is often described as a cup of wrath being poured out (Psalm 79:6; Revelation 14:10). When Jesus uses the metaphor of "cup" in the Garden of Gethsemane, it is God's wrath He has in mind. The "cup" was not just the fact that Jesus was going to die a horrible death. Rather, it was because that in that death He was taking the "cup of God's wrath" toward sin on Himself. He was, in the words of the apostle Paul, becoming sin (2 Corinthians 5:21). This is the aspect of His death that brought such anxiety on Him to produce sweat drops of blood.

things may not have turned out like you thought they would. But if you are committed to following God you can have confidence to continue on because you know He knows why things are the way they are. You can trust that He has your best interest at heart. In the end, no matter how bad the present, He will work things out for your good and His glory (Romans 8:28).

What's the alternative to placing your confidence in God's sovereignty? Would you rather place your confidence in your closest friends? Do you think they know what is best for you?

On that evening when Jesus was at His lowest, when He needed His friends the most, His friends were not there for Him. They drifted off to sleep. Matthew writes, "Then he returned to his disciples and found them sleeping. 'Could you men not keep watch with me for one hour?' he asked Peter. 'Watch and pray so that you will not fall into temptation. The spirit is willing, but the body is weak.'[3]

"He went away a second time and prayed, 'My Father, if it is not possible for this cup to be taken away unless I drink it, may your will be done.'

"When He came back, he again found them sleeping, because their eyes were heavy. So he left them and went away once more and prayed the third time, saying the same thing.

"Then He returned to the disciples and said to them, 'Are you still sleeping and resting? Look, the hour is near, and the Son of Man is betrayed into the hands of sinners. Rise, let us go! Here comes my betrayer.'" (Matthew 26:40-46).

How many times have you been struggling while your friends were sleeping? How many times have *you* been sleeping while your friend was struggling? We don't intentionally neglect our friends. But we get tired carrying our own loads. By the end of the day we have very little energy left and so we sleep. We don't pay attention. We give in to temptation. We want to be trusted. But as your friend, I am telling you not to place your complete confidence in your friends and their good intentions. Place your confidence in God's sovereignty.

Jesus also received confidence and courage because He believed God had a plan and a purpose for His life. Somehow, and in someway, being betrayed and crucified were part of His plan. He may not have like it (humanly speaking), but He knew there was a reason why He had to go through what He had to go through.

What's the alternative? Would you rather trust in the plans and purposes you have for yourself? Your plans may or may not happen. If they do, however, you will discover they were hollow and empty plans. If they don't happen, it could lead you down a path of despair and discouragement. Maybe they will happen. Maybe all the plans and dreams you have for yourself will work out. Maybe all your dreams will come true. Maybe you will live a fairytale life. And then what? You will leave this world with the same amount of stuff you brought to the world. Once you're gone, the tax collectors and funeral directors and lawyers and leeches will get all your dreams and everything you have worked so hard for. Now you understand why Jesus said what He said, "What good is it for a man to gain the whole world, yet forfeit his soul? Or what can a man give in exchange for his soul?" (Mark 8:36-37).

When you put your confidence in God's plan for your life the future looks bright no matter how dark the present may be. But when your confidence is in yourself and your dreams and plans, the future will always be in doubt.

Another way Jesus found strength and confidence was to stay focused on the eternal, not the temporal. Somehow, deep inside, even in the middle of what could be perceived as doubt, Jesus understood the big picture. He knew the only way for this cup to be taken away was to drink it. He understood that what He was doing in the present had eternal consequences.

Likewise, while this life is temporary, what we do in this life has eternal consequences. The way we stay focused, during the difficult times, is by focusing on the eternal, not the temporary. The Apostle Paul put it this way, "I consider that our present sufferings are not worth comparing with the glory that will be revealed in us" (Romans 8:18).

Once again, from a human perspective, Jesus had failed. One of his closest friends betrayed Him, He was arrested, and then after a brief skirmish, the rest of His friends "deserted him and fled" (Matthew 26:56).

Jesus was all alone. It wasn't supposed to be this way. It didn't seem life was working out the way anyone thought. But the story isn't over.

And neither is your story. Right now, things may not

make sense. Right now you may feel betrayed and all alone. But hang in there. Don't give up. God knows what He is doing. He has neither forgotten nor forsaken you. Trust in His sovereignty, in His plan for your life, and keep focused on the eternal.

---

## ENDNOTES

[1] Erik Erikson was born in Frankfurt, Germany on June 15, 1902. He died in the United States on May 12, 1994.

[2] Erikson's eight stages are as follows: (1) Infancy (trust vs. mistrust); the key event is feeding. (2) Toddlerhood (autonomy vs. doubt and shame); the key event is toilet training. (3) Preschool (initiative vs. guilt); the key event is independence. (4) Preadolescence (industriousness vs. inferiority); key event is school. (5) Adolescence (identity vs. confusion); key event is peer relationships. (6) Young Adulthood (intimacy vs. isolation); key event is love relationships. (7) Middle Adulthood (making a difference vs. self-absorption); key event is parenting. (8) Old Age (integrity vs. despair); key event is reflection on and acceptance of one's life.

[3] Don't miss this. In Matthew 26:31-35, Jesus tells Peter that he will deny Him. Peter strongly objects, saying he would die for Jesus. Now, Jesus speaks directly to Peter and warns him to stay alert or he will give in to temptation. Is it possible the temptation Jesus is referring to will be Peter's temptation to deny Him? Then, in Matthew 26:69-75, Peter denies Jesus three times! Peter did not keep watch. He fell asleep three times. He denied Jesus three times. Finally, in John 21:15-19, Jesus reinstates Peter—three times.

# Questions for Discussion

1. Have you ever experienced a time in your life when you thought that life wasn't fair and that things were not supposed to turn out the way they have? What did you do during that time? How did you stay focused? How did you keep the faith?

2. What does it mean to you to know that Jesus experienced the same type of things that you experience?

3. How would you define the word "betrayal"? Give an illustration.

4. What do you think is the significance of the fact that Jesus, while He knew Judas was going to betray Him, still let him participate in what we now call the Lord's Supper?

5. Since committing your life to Jesus, have you had any experiences that made you think, "This is not what I signed up for?"

6. Do you agree with the statement made in this chapter that Jesus did not want to die? Why or why not?

7. Three things were mentioned in this chapter that enabled Jesus to say "Not my will, but yours be done." What were those three things, and which one do you think is the most important? Why do you think it is the most important?

# 11

# The Darkest Day in History

Pastor Steve had only been at his new church three months when Sarah, one of the key lay persons, came to him with a problem. In addition to cleaning houses and volunteering at the church, Sarah kept children in her home. Months earlier, before Pastor Steve became pastor, one of the parents of one of the children had Sarah arrested for child abuse. In two weeks Sarah was going to court for a full trial and she wanted her new pastor to stand by her side.

Although he had known her for only a few months, there was no way Pastor Steve could believe Sarah was a child abuser. She taught a preschool Sunday School class and regularly worked in the nursery. He had seen her interact with children. There was no doubt in his mind this was a miscarriage of justice!

Nothing during the trial changed his mind. The evidence was weak and circumstantial. The character witnesses for Sarah were powerful. After two days of testimony the trial went to the jury. A couple of hours later the jury returned a unanimous verdict, "not guilty!"

Pastor Steve was relieved. Sarah was ecstatic. She had been completely exonerated, but the damage of the charges had been done. Regardless of her innocence, she would never keep children in her home again. Sadly, the child in question had been abused, just not by Sarah.

Betty was an outstanding fourth grade teacher in a district that boasted the best schools in the state. Betty was especially gifted with students who struggled with some of the basic concepts of reading, writing, and arithmetic. Her best quality was that she really loved her children and viewed teaching as a ministry. Word spread quickly through third grade parents that if your child was struggling, request Betty for fourth grade. She was a real miracle worker.

Because of her success, Betty's class had an unusually high percentage of "below-average" students (whatever that means). As a result, her students' scores on standardized tests were lower than the accepted average. When it came time for her annual review, she was denied tenure and lost her job. The reason for her dismissal, according to the superintendant of schools, was her failure to raise test scores to an acceptable level.

How many times in your life have you said, "that's not fair?" How many times have you been unfairly criticized, accused, or overlooked for a promotion? How many times have you wished God would make things right?

Nothing makes us angrier quicker than injustice done to ourselves or to a friend.

Once, in elementary school I was accused of stealing a boy's eraser. I hadn't stolen it. The truth is it was my eraser and he had stolen it and I was trying to get it back. But the truth didn't matter. I was sent to the principle's office. I got in trouble. No one believed me, and 35 years later I still remember the event. It takes a long time to get over a miscarriage of justice. But my experience or Betty's experience or Sarah's experience pales in comparison to the greatest injustice that has ever been done. Our justice system is built on the conviction that it is better for a guilty person to go free than for an innocent person to be condemned. Nothing is worse than an innocent person being found guilty.

But that's exactly what happened with Jesus! He was 100 percent innocent. Yet He was 100 percent found guilty. The apostle Paul put it this way, "God made Him who had no sin to be sin for us, so that in him we might become the righteousness of God" (2 Corinthians 5:21).[1]

## A Miscarriage of Justice

Nothing cries foul like an innocent man being condemned. The last week of Jesus' life started out with the greatest day in His life. On Sunday He rode into Jerusalem on the back of a colt while thousands of people shouted, "Hosanna to the Son of David! Blessed is he who comes in the name of the Lord! Hosanna in the highest!" (Matthew 21:9).

But immediately, His popularity started to polarize

people. What started out as a celebration ended as a crucifixion. Here is how it happened.

On Monday, Jesus goes into a fit of righteous anger and throws the merchants and money changers out of the temple.[2] On Tuesday, He has a confrontation with the religious leaders about the events that took place on Monday. The rest of Tuesday He spends teaching in parables.[3] On Wednesday Jesus continues teaching, giving His famous "Greatest Commandment" speech, as well as His sermon on the end of time. Wednesday evening Jesus is in the home of Lazarus where a woman anoints His feet with oil. The day ends with Judas meeting with religious leaders, negotiating the place and price of Jesus' betrayal.[4]

On Thursday, things start to climax. Judas and the authorities have their plan in place. Jesus plans on celebrating the Passover with His disciples over a meal. At the end of the meal, Jesus takes the bread and wine and uses them as an illustration of His broken body and spilled blood. Later that evening, He and His disciples go to a private garden to pray and rest. While praying, a large crowd with swords and clubs surround Jesus. Judas, the leader of the mob, betrays Jesus by kissing Him on the cheek. A skirmish occurs in which Peter cuts a guy's ear off. Jesus heals the man and says, "Am I leading a rebellion, that you have come out with swords and clubs to capture me? Every day I sat in the temple courts teaching, and you did not arrest Me" (Matthew 26:55). And then the Bible records, "Then all the disciples deserted him and fled."[5]

After being arrested, late into Thursday evening, Jesus is taken to stand trial before the Jewish religious high court (called the Sanhedrin). His charge is blasphemy. He is found guilty. The sentence for blasphemy is death. It is during this trial that Peter thrice denies being one of Jesus' disciples, even knowing Jesus.[6]

Early Friday morning, before sunrise, Jesus is taken to stand before Pilate, the Roman authority. The Jewish leaders knew that nothing (especially a death sentence) could be carried out without his approval. At first Pilate doesn't approve. He tries to release Jesus, but the crowds (the same crowd that days earlier shouted "Hosanna") now shout "Crucify Him!" Pilate washes his hands of the whole ugly event and then turns Jesus over to the Roman soldiers who beat Him, mock Him, and prepare Him for crucifixion.[7]

More than likely, within twelve hours of His arrest, Jesus was beaten, bruised, and hung on a cross . . . and He was completely innocent of any criminal or religious charges! An incredible display of incompetence, hatred, apathy, and injustice.

How could such a thing happen? It's called "groupthink," where bad (sometimes unspeakable) ideas become acceptable ideas as a result of people conforming to someone's agenda. Groupthink often leads to a herd mentality, where people simply follow along without questioning why. The religious leaders, with their hidden agenda of getting rid of Jesus, manipulated the populace and the Roman authorities into accepting what, under normal circumstances, would have been unacceptable.

The Sanhedrin also violated 24 Jewish laws in the way they treated Jesus. Among those violations were condemning the accused on the same day as the trial. It was also against Jewish law to deal with a capital punishment case at night. A third violation was pronouncing a death penalty outside a specially called meeting in the temple. Furthermore, a trial was not to be held on the eve of the Sabbath or the eve of a festival day. (The day Jesus was arrested, tried, and condemned was the eve of the Passover.) Another violation was not allowing the defense an opportunity to call witnesses on his behalf.

Could such a travesty happen today?

Think about it, and be honest: How many times have you seen someone arrested and immediately presumed he (or she) must have done something wrong or else he (or she) would not have been arrested? A person is supposed to have the presumption of innocence. But we put so much trust in the authorities, and groupthink is so powerful, people have to *prove* their innocence instead of *disprove* their guilt. We can't judge the people of Jesus' day because many of us would have probably done the same thing.

Here is how Matthew describes what happens next:

*As they were going out, they met a man from Cyrene, named Simon, and they forced him to carry the cross. They came to a place called Golgotha (which means The Place of the Skull). There they offered Jesus wine to drink, mixed with gall; but after tasting it, he refused to drink it. When they had crucified him, they divided up his clothes by casting lots. And sitting down, they kept watch over him there. Above his head they placed the written charge against him: THIS IS JESUS, THE KING OF THE JEWS. Two robbers were crucified with him, one on his right and one on his left. Those who passed by hurled insults at him, shaking their heads and saying, "You who are going to destroy the temple and build it in three days, save yourself! Come down from the cross, if you are the Son of God!"*

*In the same way the chief priests, the teachers of the law and the elders mocked him. "He saved others," they said, "but he can't save himself! He's the King of Israel! Let him come down now from the cross, and we will believe in him. He trusts in God. Let God rescue him now if he wants him, for he said, 'I am the Son of God.' "In the same way the robbers who were crucified with him also heaped insults on him"* (Matthew 27:32-44).

Mark records that Jesus was crucified during the "third hour," (Mark 15:25) which was 9:00 a.m. Friday. However, He did not die right away. Death would take hours. And as He hung on the cross it would be easy to conclude He was a failure. How could things have gone so wrong?

## A Loss of Hope

Chances are you have heard the gory details of the crucifixion so many times you have become numb to it. Yes, it happened. Yes, it was horrible. Yes, it was unthinkable. Yes, it was unimaginable. But we convince ourselves that it is simply part of the story. We know how the story ends and so we gloss over the atrocity of it all. After all, it's Friday, but Sunday's coming, right?

Let's not be so quick to get to Sunday that we miss some incredible, life-changing principles. Before we jump to His resurrection, what are some principles we can learn from Jesus' crucifixion?

Remember, Jesus was as much human as He was God. As a human being He experienced every temptation and every emotion you and I have ever experienced. He knows how you feel because He has felt it. Yes, He is God, and yes, He did overcome everything. That means He can sympathize with you and give you the strength to overcome as well.

Have you ever had a bad day? I mean a really bad day? Not a bad hair day, or just a rotten day when nothing seemed to go right and you were in a really foul mood. I mean a really, really bad day?

Do you know how you can tell when you are really having a bad day?

First, you know you are having a bad day when your enemies want to crucify you. I know a guy who pastored a church, who was at a business meeting that went terribly wrong. At one point in the meeting, a man (who happened to be a deacon and the church treasurer) said to the pastor, in front of everyone, "I don't have any respect for you as a pastor or as a man."

It's one thing to be around people and *wonder* if they like you or not. But it's another thing to be around people and *know* they don't like you. Jesus knew who His enemies were, He knew who wanted Him dead, and in the Garden of Gethsemane, those were the people who surrounded Him. It's a bad day when someone wants you dead.[8]

Second, you know you are having a bad day when your friends desert you. Judas betrayed Jesus with a kiss. But in a flash the rest of the disciples ran away. It's a miserable feeling to be in a position where you need your friends, but they are not there.

Third, you know you are having a bad day when you can't see a brighter tomorrow. As long as you can say—if I just hold on a little longer, I know it will get better—you can find the strength to keep going. It's another thing to lose all hope of things ever getting better. Matthew records, "From the sixth hour [noon] until the ninth hour [3:00 p.m., and remember Jesus had been on the cross since 9:00 a.m.] darkness came over all the land" (Matthew 27:45).

Will the sun (or Son) really come out tomorrow? When you doubt it will, that's a really bad day.

Fourth, you know you are having a bad day when your religion no longer provides adequate answers. Jesus cried, "My God, my God, why have you forsaken me?" (Matthew 27:46).

God doesn't answer.

Have you ever been in a situation when what you believed all your life no longer answered your questions in any real and meaningful way? It's a bad day when that happens. It is tough to pour out your soul to God and God seem like He no longer cares, if He ever cared at all.

Fifth, you know you are having a bad day when your life is being slowly squeezed out of you. It could be financial pressures, family pressures, work pressures, or just about any type of stress. It's hard to keep going when you feel like you are dying.

## Now What?

Now, here is the good news. While Jesus' enemies wanted to kill Him, and while His friends deserted Him, and while there seemed to be no brighter tomorrow, and while His religion no longer had the answers, and while His life was slowly leaving Him, God was up to something! God had not forgotten His promises. He had not forsaken His Son. He had not fallen asleep at the wheel.

It may seem as if He had failed, but God was up to something huge! He was up to something that would change everything and make everything worthwhile.

At the precise moment Jesus died, the curtain in the temple that separated the Holy of Holies (where God resided) from the rest of the temple was torn in two from top to bottom (Mathew 27:51).

What does that mean? In the temple there was a room where the ark of the covenant was kept. God dwelt in the ark of the covenant. This room was the most holy room in

131

the temple. Indeed it was the most holy room in the world. Once a year the high priest, and only the high priest, went into this room with a sacrifice and asked God to forgive the sins of the people. If other people went into the room, at any time, they were immediately struck dead by God. If the high priest went into this room on any day but the one day a year, he would be struck dead. No exceptions. If there was any unconfessed sin in the life of the high priest, the moment he walked into the room he died. The priests were not perfect. Any time he walked into this room there was a chance he would die. As a precaution, before entering the room, on this one day a year, the high priest tied a rope around his waist, leaving the slack in the rope outside the Holy of Holies. This way, if the priest died, other priests could drag him out of the room without being killed themselves.

This holy room was separated from the rest of the temple by a huge, heavy curtain. The curtain was woven fabric of 72 twisted plaits of 24 threads each and was 60 feet long by 30 feet high. Only God could split it from top to bottom.

The ripping of this veil signified that God was now entering into a new, open relationship with humanity. Now, at anytime, anyone could go to God for forgiveness. No priest was necessary. No sacrifices were necessary. No appointment needed. The moment Jesus died, God declared that through Jesus all sins could be forgiven and through Jesus everyone is welcomed into His presence. "Therefore, brothers, since we have confidence to enter the Most Holy Place by the blood of Jesus, by a new and living way opened for us through the curtain, that is, his body, and since we have a great priest over the house of God, let us draw near to God with a sincere heart in full assurance of faith, having our hearts sprinkled to cleanse us from a guilty conscience and having our bodies washed with pure water" (Hebrews 10:19-22).

Some other unusual things happened while the temple veil was being ripped: "The earth shook and the rocks split. The tombs broke open and the bodies of many holy people who had died were raised to life" (Matthew 27:51-52). All were signs that God accepted Jesus' death as the sacrifice for sins. Nothing would ever be the same again. At the darkest moment imaginable, God was up to something.

## Turning a Bad Day into a Good Day

I have a friend, a retired minister, who recently died of cancer. This man meant the world to me. Over the last few months of his life he has had several bad days, but it seemed the worse his days, the stronger his faith. He was always smiling. While taking chemo, he talked to the doctors, nurses, and other patients about Jesus. He even prayed with them. Several of those patients attended his funeral. Through it all he was an encouragement to me and everyone who met him. I pray that on my good days my faith will be half as strong as his faith was on his bad days.

If you were to ask him how he kept going while life was slowly being squeezed out of him, he would have told you, "When life is at its worst, God is at His best."

That's the lesson behind the crucifixion!

That's the anchor we tether ourselves to during storms.

That's the promise to which we never let go.

That's how you keep going when you would rather quit.

That's how the darkest day in history became the greatest day ever.

That's how you turn a bad day (no matter how bad of a day) into a good day.

## ENDNOTES

[1] 2 Corinthians 5:21. *The Message* reads, "God put the wrong on Him who never did anything wrong, so we could be put right with God."

[2] Matthew 21:12-16; Mark 11:15-18; Luke 19:45-47.

[3] Matthew 21:23—22:14; Mark 11:27—12:12; Luke 20:1-19.

[4] Matthew 22:15—26:16; Mark 12:15—14:11; Luke 20:20—22:6.

[5] Matthew 26:17-56; Mark 14:12-52; Luke 22:7-53.

[6] Matthew 26:57-75; Mark 14:53-72; Luke 22:54-62.

[7] Matthew 27:11-44; Mark 15:1-32; Luke 22:63—23:43.

[8] Can you not think of an enemy who wants you dead? I can. His name is Lucifer and the Bible says he prowls around like a roaring lion looking for people to devour (1 Peter 5:8).

## Questions for Discussion

1.  Can you think of a time in your life where you thought you were treated unfairly? How did that make you feel? Can you think of a time when you saw a miscarriage of justice happen to someone around you? How did you react?

2.  Go over, and discuss, what happened on each day of the last week of Jesus' life. How does an understanding of these events change your view of the crucifixion?

3.  Compare Judas' betrayal of Jesus with a kiss, to the disciples deserting Jesus after His arrest, and Peter's denial of Jesus during Jesus' trial. Which betrayal is worse? Why?

4.  According to this chapter, what are the five ways you can know you are having a bad day? How do those ways apply to your life? Have you had an experience with each of those ways?

5.  According to the chapter, how do you turn a bad day into a good day? How does knowing that simple truth apply to your life?

# 12

# That's the End of That

What do you do when you don't know what to do? Where do you look for answers when life seems to ask unanswerable questions? Where do you turn when all hope seems lost? What do you do when your dreams turn to nightmares?

Several years ago a matriarch of the church I was pastoring was losing a painful battle to cancer. She fought valiantly, but it was painfully clear she was losing. Death could come at any moment. Hospice had been called to the house and I stayed in constant contact with the family.

The news came with a mid-morning phone call. I knew the voice on the other end was a daughter of the matriarch, and so I braced myself for the certain news of her passing. Hardly able to speak, the voice on the other end said, "Kevin, he's gone. I can't believe he is gone. What are we going to do?"

Confused, I said, "What? Who's gone? What's happened? Has Mrs. Rutledge died?"

"No Kevin, it's not mom; it's Johnny. He has been killed."

Johnny was Mrs. Rutledge's ten year old great-grandson. That morning, while waiting for his school bus, a dump truck swerved, lost control, and ran over him, killing him instantly. Instead of planning a funeral for someone who had lived a long life, I was now planning a funeral for a young child.

"Kevin," the painful voice cried, "Why did God allow this to happen?"

I had no answer. There was no answer. A few days after Johnny's funeral, I stood beside Mrs. Rutledge's casket and cried. I still had no answer. To this day, I have no answer. The blank stares on some of the family made it clear they had lost hope. How could they pick up the pieces and keep going?

I imagine Jesus' disciples had the same sense of hopelessness after Jesus was arrested. I imagine His mother felt hopeless as she looked up at Jesus hanging on a cross while blood poured from His hands, feet, and side.

Things looked hopeless.

But things were about to change. Nothing was ever going to be the same again.

## You Can't Keep a Good Man Down

One week earlier, Jesus was treated to a parade fit for a king, or the Super Bowl champions, or the World Series victors. By the following Friday the world was dark, the disciples were scared, and Jesus was being tortured. All hope seemed lost. But by early Sunday morning things were incredibly different. Not much had changed. Rome was still in charge. The disciples were still fearful for their own lives, an injustice like nothing in all of history, had still been carried out on an innocent man. But while it seemed not much had changed, everything had changed! Jesus was alive and that meant there was hope. Listen to how Matthew tells the story:

*After the Sabbath, at dawn on the first day of the week, Mary Magdalene and the other Mary went to look at the tomb.*

*There was a violent earthquake, for an angel of the Lord came down from heaven and, going to the tomb, rolled back the stone and sat on it. His appearance was like lightning, and his clothes were white as snow. The guards were so afraid of him that they shook and became like dead men.*

*The angel said to the women, "Do not be afraid, for I know that you are looking for Jesus, who was crucified. He is not here; he has risen, just as he said. Come and see the place where he lay. Then go quickly and tell his disciples: 'He has risen from the dead and is going ahead of you into Galilee. There you will see him.' Now I have told you."*

*So the women hurried away from the tomb, afraid yet filled with joy, and ran to tell his disciples. Suddenly Jesus met them. "Greetings," he said. They came to him, clasped his feet and worshiped him. Then Jesus said to them, "Do not be afraid. Go and tell my brothers to go to Galilee; there they will see me"* (Matthew 28:1-10).

The way Jews kept time in Jesus' day is different than the

way we keep time. For example, if the crucifixion happened today and Jesus died on Friday and then appeared alive on Sunday, we would say He had been dead two days . . . Saturday and Sunday. However, in Jesus' day, any part of a day was counted as a day. Also, in Judaism, a new day started at 6:00 p.m. Jesus died sometime around 3:00 p.m. Friday. The Sabbath, Saturday, began at 6:00 p.m. Friday. Thus, the three hours Jesus was dead on Friday afternoon would have counted as day one.

Jesus was in the tomb the entire second day from 6:00 p.m. Friday to 6:00 p.m. Saturday. The third day, the day on which Jesus rose from the dead, would have begun at 6:00 p.m. Saturday. Matthew says the ladies went to the tomb at "dawn" Sunday morning. John says it was so early in the morning it was still dark (John 20:1). Sometime between 6:00 p.m. Saturday evening and 6:00 a.m. Sunday morning, Jesus' resurrection took place.

Matthew tells us that the first witnesses to the resurrection were women. These women, Mary Magdalene and another woman named Mary, were the same women who cried at the foot of the cross while Jesus was dying (Matthew 27:56).[1] It was the custom of the day for family and friends to visit the tombs of loved ones until the third day to make sure the deceased were really dead and to anoint them with oils. The ladies would not have visited the tomb during the Sabbath, so they were anxious to go Sunday morning and continue the grieving process. In no way were they expecting what they encountered. Their expectation was to see Jesus' dead body in the tomb.

Palestine sits on a fault zone[2] and is prone to earthquakes. I imagine that while the ladies walked to the tomb a violent earthquake shook the earth. God used the earthquake to roll the stone away from the entrance to the tomb.[3] Along with the earthquake, an angel came down and sat on the stone, terrifying the guards so much they fainted in fear. Usually, tombs were not guarded by Roman soldiers, especially tombs of accused criminals, which is what Jesus was. The religious leaders requested this action out of fear that Jesus'

"Many scholars consider God's choice of women as the first witnesses of Jesus' resurrection to be one of the bedrock truths of the resurrection narratives and the historicity of the resurrection itself. It is unlikely that any Jew would have created such a story as fiction, for a variety of reasons. (1) Because of the debated status of a woman in Judaism at the time, there was disagreement among some of the rabbis as to the acceptability of a woman giving testimony in a court of law. This would make it much less likely that a Jew would fictionalize a woman's testimony in the case of Jesus' resurrection. (2) The cowardly picture painted of the men hiding away in Jerusalem, while the women boldly carry out their responsibilities to prepare Jesus' body for burial, would certainly offend the sensibilities of Jewish readers and doubtless would not have been recorded unless it were true. (3) The listing of the names of the women weighs against being fiction, because these women were known in early Christian fellowship and would not have easily been associated with a false account. (4) Jesus' appearances to these women with debated status lend credibility to the account, because again, they would be unlikely selections for a fictionalized account trying to be understood as believable.

For these reasons and more, the selection of women as the first witnesses yields high credibility to the resurrection narratives and the resurrection itself. It is vitally important for us to build our faith on the solid foundation of the historically verifiable truth of the resurrection of Jesus Christ." (Clinton E. Arnold, General Editor. 2002. *Zondervan Illustrated Bible Backgrounds Commentary,* vol. 1. Grand Rapids, MI: Zondervan Publishing House, p. 188.)

disciples would try to steal the body and claim He had risen from the dead.

There is nothing in the story to suggest the ladies knew there would be guards present, or that they saw these events actually take place. All Matthew says is that when they arrived at the tomb, the angel tells them Jesus is alive and invites them to go into the tomb and look for themselves. Mark describes the angel as a "young man dressed in a white robe" (Mark 16:5).[4] He looked like a normal person except for how he was dressed.

Convinced Jesus was alive, the ladies hurried to tell the disciples. Somewhere along the way, they were greeted by Jesus and immediately fell down to worship Him. Hope, which had been crucified, was now brought back to life! Jesus' seemingly great failure, was in actuality his greatest success.

*The resurrection equals hope!* That's it, nothing more and nothing less, everything else that has been preached and written flow out of that one simple truth. Because Jesus is alive there is hope.

Like everything else in our society, Easter has been commercialized. Easter marks the beginning of spring. It's a chance to hunt for eggs filled with candy and to buy new clothes. It's an opportunity to send cards to friends and to eat chocolate. It's a day for families to go to church and then go home for a wonderful Easter lunch. It means a long weekend and possibly a spring vacation. Easter is a wonderful time. I enjoy all those trappings of the secular side of Easter. I don't condemn any of those practices. I simply think that we need to constantly remind ourselves that above and beyond all those things, Easter is about hope, and the proper response to the hope we have in Jesus is to stop what we are doing and worship the One who gives us hope, just like the ladies did on that first Easter morning.

## Hope

As a pastor I have performed many funeral services. Although they are never easy, there is a stark contrast between funerals of believers and funerals of non-believers. I have been involved in funerals that seemed more like a party than a death, and I have been involved in funerals that seemed so dark you didn't know if the bereaved would ever overcome the grief. I have been to funerals where there was more laughter than tears and ones where the sorrow was so heavy it was hard to bare.

I am convinced, however, that the difference in the funerals I have participated in is a difference of hope. Some people have it; others' don't. When you have experienced hope, you have experienced the same thing the ladies experienced on that first Easter morning: "afraid yet filled with joy" (Matthew 28:8). Hope doesn't remove you from the present circumstance. Hope helps you see above and beyond the present circumstance. Hope isn't being naïve. Hope is being confident that God is in control even when things are chaotic. Hope isn't living in denial. Hope is living in the reality that God is sovereign. Hope, however, extends before and beyond the grave.

First, because of the resurrection of Jesus Christ we have hope of a redeemed past.

Have you ever had a dream that was so bad and so real, when you woke up and realized it was all a dream, you felt relieved? Don't you wish real life was like that? Don't you wish you could go back and do things differently? All of us have things in our past we wish were not there.

Here is the good news: *Because Jesus is alive He can reach back and make our past right.* It's called grace, and it's more than forgiving and forgetting; it's taking our past and turning it around and upside down, using it to make us who we are today. No matter how invaluable, corrupt, or abusive our past may have been, through Jesus, God forgives it, forgets about it in the sense He no longer holds it against us, and uses it to make us valuable and incorruptible. Listen to these words of the apostle Paul:

*And we know that in all things God works for the good of those who love him, who have been called according to his purpose. For those God foreknew he also predestined to be conformed to the likeness of his Son, that he might be the firstborn among many brothers. And those he predestined, he also called; those he called, he also justified; those he justified, he also glorified.*

*What, then, shall we say in response to this? If God is for us, who can be against us? He who did not spare his own Son, but gave him up for us all—how will he not also, along with him, graciously give us all things? Who will bring any charge against those whom God has chosen? It is God who justifies. Who is he that condemns? Christ Jesus, who died—more than that, who was raised to life—is at the right hand of God and is also interceding for us. Who shall separate us from the love of Christ? Shall trouble or hardship or persecution or famine or nakedness or danger or sword? [36] As it is written: "For your sake we face death all day long; we are considered as sheep to be slaughtered."*

*No, in all these things we are more than conquerors through him who loved us. For I am convinced that neither death nor life, neither angels nor demons, neither the present nor the future, nor any powers, neither height nor depth, nor anything else in all creation, will be able to separate us from the love of God that is in Christ Jesus our Lord* (Romans 8:28-39).

Secondly, because of the resurrection of Jesus Christ, we have hope of a meaningful present.

Jesus told the ladies, "Go and tell my brothers to go to Galilee; there they will see me" (Matthew 28:10). Though they were afraid, and though Mark says at first they did not tell anyone (Mark 16:8), eventually they could hold the news no longer. Luke says they told the disciples Jesus was alive, but the disciples did not believe them. After all, it made no sense, and women were not considered credible sources in those days.[5]

Peter wanted to check out the story for himself, so he ran to the tomb. Eventually all the disciples believed and were witnesses of His resurrected body, and the group that once feared for its life became filled with confidence and changed their world. They spent the rest of their lives traveling the world, telling others about the resurrected Jesus. As a result of their zeal, most of them died as horrible a death as Jesus did. But none of that mattered. Jesus was alive! Now they had a reason to live. Now their lives made sense. Now there was a purpose for the present.

Once your past is redeemed, your present takes on new

meaning. You are a child of God! God has a purpose and a plan for your life. There is a reason you are where you are, doing what you are doing. Your life makes sense. Your life has meaning. Today is another day to live for Him. Today is another day to share the love of Christ with those around you. You have been forgiven to forgive. You have been loved to love. You have been redeemed to share redemption with others.

Finally, because of the resurrection of Jesus Christ we have hope of a brighter tomorrow.

The apostle Paul put it this way:

*But if it is preached that Christ has been raised from the dead, how can some of you say that there is no resurrection of the dead? If there is no resurrection of the dead, then not even Christ has been raised. And if Christ has not been raised, our preaching is useless and so is your faith. More than that, we are then found to be false witnesses about God, for we have testified about God that he raised Christ from the dead. But he did not raise him if in fact the dead are not raised. For if the dead are not raised, then Christ has not been raised either. And if Christ has not been raised, your faith is futile; you are still in your sins. Then those also who have fallen asleep in Christ are lost. If only for this life we have hope in Christ, we are to be pitied more than all men.*

*But Christ has indeed been raised from the dead, the firstfruits of those who have fallen asleep. For since death came through a man, the resurrection of the dead comes also through a man. For as in Adam all die, so in Christ all will be made alive* (1 Corinthians 15:12-22).[6]

No matter how bad things may be right now, in Christ there is hope for a brighter and better tomorrow. Paul remind us, "I consider that our present sufferings are not worth comparing with the glory that will be revealed in us" (Romans 8:18). Just like today, whatever you are facing is temporary. Life is temporary. Things will get better. The sun will shine tomorrow. In Jesus we have eternal and abundant life.

The meaning of the resurrection is hope that compels

me to worship the risen Christ. The hope Jesus brings is the hope of a redeemed past, a meaningful present, and a brighter tomorrow.

One day a friend of mine, an older gentleman, was asked what he wanted people to say at his funeral. His response was classic. He said, "I want them to say, 'Look, he's moving.'"

Have you ever known of someone who died and then came back to life? I am not talking about a near death experience, or an experience of seeing a bright light. I mean dead—dead for a few days—and then they come back to life. Have you ever, in your lifetime, experienced such a thing?

I have . . . well, sort of. Let me explain.

It was a Thanksgiving morning. Our neighbor from across the street knocked on our door in a panic. Frantically, she told me that her friend's teenage daughter was involved in a terrible automobile accident. Her daughter's friend was in intensive care at a local hospital. Another teenage girl was driving, and she had been killed.

I immediately went to the hospital. The mom was nearly inconsolable. Her daughter had tubes running all through her. Things did not look good. The mom was also upset about the other girl who had died, but was relieved her daughter had survived. I said I would go to the funeral home to see the other family. Before I left the hospital, I had prayer with the girl and her mom.

Two days later, this time in late afternoon, my neighbor banged on the door again. There had been a mistake. The girl in the hospital was not her friend's daughter. Her friend's daughter was the girl who had been killed; and the family who thought their daughter was dead was the girl in the hospital, alive and well enough to write her real name on a note pad. It was a bizarre case of mistaken identity. I performed the funeral for the deceased, spoke at a memorial service at the local high school, ministered to the family of the girl who survived, and was interviewed by *Inside Edition*. It was a crazy time to say the least.

It is obvious how the mom felt, who thought her child

was alive, only to discover her child had died. But can you imagine how the other family felt? They were at the funeral home, preparing to receive visitors, with no hope of ever talking to their child again, when they learned their daughter was alive! I can't imagine the range of emotions they must have gone through during those few days.

I imagine Jesus' mother went through the same emotions. One day you feel hopeless, and the next day hope is alive. I imagine Jesus' disciples felt the same way. Now, because Jesus was alive, all the past made sense, the present takes on new meaning, and tomorrow will be better than today. That's the hope Easter brings.

Do you have that hope, or are you still dealing with the pain of the past?

Do you have that hope, or are you barely hanging on, trying to make it through one more day?

Do you have that hope, or are you afraid to face the future?

In Jesus Christ, and through Jesus Christ, there is always hope for everything.

# ENDNOTES

[1] In Matthew 27:56 the "other Mary" is identified as "Mary the mother of James and Joses." Taking all four gospels into account, the women who attended to Jesus at the cross and who visited the tomb were Mary Magdalene, Mary the mother of James and Joses, Salome the mother of James and John, Mary the mother of Jesus, Joanna the wife of Chuza, Suzanne, and several unnamed women.

[2] The "Jordan Valley Rift is part of a large fault zone that stretches northward from the entrance of the Gulf of Aqaba for over 683 miles to the foot of the Taurus range" (Clinton E. Arnold, General Editor. 2002. *Zondervan Illustrated Bible Background Commentary*, vol. 1. Grand Rapids, MI: Zondervan Publishing House, p. 185. Used by permission of Zondervan.

[3] It has been widely observed that the stone was rolled away, not to let Jesus out, but to let the women in.

[4] Mark also suggests that by the time the ladies got to the grave site, the angels were not sitting on the stone, but were inside the tomb.

[5] Luke 24:11. In Jesus' day, women had low social standing. Women's testimonies were not deemed worthy to be used in court. The very fact Jesus first appeared to women shows His willingness to break with the norms of the day.

[6] 1 Corinthians 15:12-22.

# Questions for Discussion

1.  Describe a time in your life when you felt completely helpless, not knowing what to do? Have you ever questioned God? Have you ever experienced a time when you felt there was no hope? How did you handle that time?

2.  Using commentaries, the internet, and other references, research the role of women in Jesus' day and use that to start a discussion on the importance of Jesus showing Himself alive to women first. What is the implication of this?

3.  The resurrection equals hope. How would you define hope? How would you explain the hope of the resurrection to someone else?

4.  The hope of the resurrection redeems our past, gives our present meaning and purpose, and promises us a brighter tomorrow. How does the resurrection redeem our past? How does the resurrection give meaning and purpose to our present? How does the resurrection promise us a brighter tomorrow?

5.  Based on your responses to question #4, which resurrection hope do you think is the most important? Why?

# 13

# Now It's
# Your Turn

### "Jesus is alive!"[1]

"Yea, Nate, I can feel His presence. It's like He's watching over us. I know it's up to you, me, and the others to keep His memory and His message alive. I just don't know if I have the ability. I don't know if it's worth risking my life."

"No, Tommy, you don't understand," Nate insisted. "Jesus is really, physically alive."

"What? Have you lost your mind? There's no way He's alive. You heard His mother describe the pain and torture of His death. You know about the spear being thrown into His side," Tommy protested.

"Listen to me, Tommy," Nate continued. "Jesus is alive! Mary Magdalene and some other women went to the tomb this morning to anoint His body. Did you feel the earthquake this morning? It could have been the earthquake, or it could have been something else, but when the ladies got to the tomb, the huge stone in front of Jesus' grave had been rolled away. The two soldiers guarding the tomb were on the ground, passed out from something, and a young man told the women Jesus was alive. He even invited them into the tomb to see for themselves. And then, as the women were leaving, Jesus showed up, talked to them, and instructed them to tell us He would meet us in Galilee. So let's go. We have to hurry. Jesus is alive!"[2]

"Nate. You know how emotional women can be. You can't trust what they say. I would be careful taking their word for it," Tom said, reflecting the cultural bias of his day.

"Maybe so," Nate continued. "That's how most of us felt. But after Peter heard the news, he ran as fast as he could to see for himself. The tomb was empty, just like Mary had said."

"Somebody must have stolen His body and . . ."

"No!" Nate interrupted. "Later in the afternoon, Cleo and his wife[3] were on their way home from Jerusalem and Jesus appeared to them. At first they did not recognize Him and assumed He was just another traveler. They asked Him to stay at their home for dinner. After dinner—Tommy, brace yourself for what I am about to say—this Stranger took bread, gave thanks, and broke it. Does that sound familiar? Immediately Cleo and his wife recognized the Stranger to be Jesus and worshiped Him."

"Wow! Coming from anyone else I would have a hard time believing it, but Cleo is a good man," Tommy admitted.

"And then, later that night, while everyone was together, everyone but you, Jesus walked right into the room. Tommy, He's alive! I swear He's alive! I have seen Him myself! You have got to believe me," pleaded Nate. "Let's hurry and get to Galilee!"

Tommy said, "Nate, I desperately want to believe you, but 'unless I see the nail marks in his hands and put my finger where the nails were, and put my hand into his side, I will not believe it.'[4] I do not want to be disappointed again! I don't think my heart would survive if this turned out untrue. You better go on to Galilee without me. I just can't do it. Not right now."

One week later, while all the disciples, including Nate and Tommy, were together, Jesus walked through a locked door, stood in the middle of the room, and said, "Peace be with you! . . . [and then to Tommy] Put your finger here; see my hands. Reach out your hand and put it into my side. Stop doubting and believe" (John 20:26-27).

## A Busy Forty Days

Jesus was killed on Friday. On Sunday, He walked out of the tomb, and over the next 40 days hundreds of people saw Him and testified that He was indeed alive.

What did Jesus do over these 40 days? Luke writes that He "gave many convincing proofs that he was alive" and taught "about the kingdom of God" (Acts 1:3). Jesus began His ministry announcing "The kingdom of God is near"

(Mark 1:15), and He continued that message until the day He left the earth. It only stands to reason that before we, His followers, do anything else, we must proclaim the message of the kingdom of God.

What were the "convincing proofs"? To Luke, a medical doctor, the most convincing proof that Jesus really was alive was that you could touch Him and feel flesh and bone; and that He asked for food and ate it in front of them (Luke 24:37-43). (A "spirit" or a delusion cannot be felt and does not eat.)

In addition to eating with His disciples and teaching them about the kingdom of God, Jesus also used these 40 days to explain, through Scripture, how all the events of His life, death, and resurrection fit together.[5] On this side of Easter, all of Scripture makes sense.

But all good things must come to an end. The theological word for this end is *ascension,* meaning "to be taken up." The *Ascension of Christ* refers to the time, 40 days after His resurrection, when Jesus was "taken up" from the disciples back to heaven where He now sits at the right hand of God.

Here is how Luke records this event: "When he had led them out to the vicinity of Bethany, he lifted up his hands and blessed them. While he was blessing them, he left them and was *taken up* into heaven" (Luke 24:50-51).[6]

In Acts, Luke goes into greater detail:

On one occasion, while he was eating with them, he gave them this command: *"Do not leave Jerusalem, but wait for the gift my Father promised, which you have heard me speak about. For John baptized with water, but in a few days you will be baptized with the Holy Spirit."*

*So when they met together, they asked him, "Lord, are you at this time going to restore the kingdom to Israel?"*

*He said to them: "It is not for you to know the times or dates the Father has set by his own authority. But you will receive power when the Holy Spirit comes on you; and you will be my witnesses in Jerusalem, and in all Judea and Samaria, and to the ends of the earth."*

*After he said this, he was taken up before their very eyes, and a cloud hid him from their sight.*

149

*They were looking intently up into the sky as he was going, when suddenly two men dressed in white stood beside them. "Men of Galilee," they said, "why do you stand here looking into the sky? This same Jesus, who has been taken from you into heaven, will come back in the same way you have seen him go into heaven"* (Acts 1:4-11).

To put the ascension into proper context, it is also important to remember part of the discussion Jesus had with His disciples on the night He was betrayed. Jesus was trying to comfort them. He was telling them He was going to have to go away and while He was gone their job (and our job) was to continue what Jesus had been doing. He said to His followers, "I tell you the truth, anyone who has faith in me will do what I have been doing. *He will do even greater things than these,* because I am going to the Father" (John 14:12).

Let those words sink in. Jesus said that once He was gone, a prophecy about both His death and ascension, His followers would continue doing what He was doing, only with greater success and greater impact! Greater success than healing the blind and the deaf! Greater success than casting out demons and raising the dead! Greater impact than feeding thousands of people with nothing more than a few fish and a few biscuits. Greater success and impact than He had!

I don't understand how such a thing is even conceivable, but I do understand this: *You and I have the potential within us to continue the ministry of Jesus in a greater magnitude than Jesus Himself.*

How is that possible? It is possible through the power of the Holy Spirit!

The "gift my Father promised" (Acts 1:4) was the gift of the Holy Spirit. Jesus told His disciples, "All this I have spoken while still with you. But the Counselor, the Holy Spirit, whom the Father will send in my name, will teach you all things and will remind you of everything I have said to you" (John 14:25-26).

On the day Jesus ascended into heaven, He blessed His disciples, telling them to go to Jerusalem and wait for the

Holy Spirit, saying to them "But you will receive power when the Holy Spirit comes on you; and you will be my witnesses in Jerusalem, and in all Judea and Samaria, and to the ends of the earth" (Acts 1:8). And while He was saying these things, He was "taken up" into heaven with a promise that He would return the same way.

## It's Our Turn

Jesus came to earth with a purpose. He had a mission to accomplish. He fulfilled His mission and now says to you and me: "It's your turn. You have a purpose and a mission."

Jesus, through the power of the Holy Spirit, has released you and me to be the best we can be. He has given us the authority to continue His ministry, and He has promised that we can do greater things then He did. "Now to him who is able to do immeasurably more than all we ask or imagine, according to his power that is at work within us, to him be glory in the church and in Christ Jesus throughout all generations for ever and ever! Amen" (Ephesians 3:20-21).

On the one hand we have all this God-given potential; but on the other hand many of us don't live up to that potential. Jesus wants us to succeed. He wants us to reach our full potential. He wants us to be the best we can be. He wants us to live a full and abundant life. But it doesn't happen automatically. There are some things we can to do in order to be all God wants us to be. What are those things? How do we reach our fullest potential? How do we continue the ministry Jesus began?

## 1. CONFESS FAITH IN THE RESURRECTED JESUS.

After Jesus was arrested His disciples ran away and hid, afraid they would be next. They only reached their potential; they only fulfilled their destiny, after they met with, and placed their faith in, the resurrected Jesus.

There is one thing absolutely essential to the Christian faith–that Jesus actually died and actually rose again. The Bible says that the one thing you must confess is that

Jesus is alive. Listen to the words of Paul, "That if you confess with your mouth, 'Jesus is Lord,' and believe in your heart that God raised him from the dead, you will be saved." (Romans 12:9).

To be "saved" literally means "to be made whole again." It refers to being brought back into a right relationship with God, so you can live in right relationship with yourself and others. It refers to being made whole again physically, spiritually, and emotionally. It means to be able to be what you were created to be, to fulfill your purpose, to be all you can be. And notice, this happens through faith in the resurrected Jesus.

## 2. SEEK RECONCILIATION WITH OTHERS.

Once you have been brought back into a right relationship with God, you have the responsibility to seek reconciliation with others. Jesus illustrates this fact beautifully in an event that happened between His resurrection and ascension.

On the evening Jesus was betrayed, He prophesied Judas would betray Him. But He also prophesied that Peter would betray Him. Judas betrayed Jesus once. Peter betrayed Him three times. After his third betrayal, Luke writes, "The Lord turned and looked straight at Peter. Then Peter remembered the word the Lord had spoken to him: 'Before the rooster crows today, you will disown me three times.' And he went outside and wept bitterly" (Luke 22:61-62).

There is no doubt Peter was remorseful for what he had done. He, maybe more than any of the other disciples, hurt when Jesus was killed. I am sure he wished he could have had one more conversation with Jesus. Just one chance to say he was sorry. He was going to have to live with this guilt his whole life. Maybe this is why he bolted from the house and ran to the tomb when he heard that Jesus wasn't there. He desperately wanted Him to be alive (Luke 14:12).

Have you ever had an argument with someone you loved, or wronged a friend, or had a good relationship ruined over a disagreement or misunderstanding? In those situations, even when you want to be reconciled, it's hard to go back to the way things were, isn't it? Sometimes it's difficult to even be in the same room with the other person. I imagine Peter desperately wanted to make things right. He just didn't know how, and when he was around Jesus, he didn't know what to say. The relationship with his dear Friend was strained.

Then, one morning, after a wasted night of fishing, from the shore Jesus told His friends to throw their nets on the other side of the boat. They did, and caught more fish then they could handle. Jesus then took some of the fish they had caught and prepared breakfast.

After breakfast, Jesus had the following conversation with Peter.[7]

"Peter, do you love Me more than fishing?"

Jesus asked him this question because Peter, along with some of the other disciples, had decided to go back into the fishing business.[8]

"Of course, I love You. You know that," Peter said.

"Then give up your dreams for your life for My dreams for your life," said Jesus.

After a few moments had gone by, Jesus again asked Peter, "Do you really love Me?"

Peter again said yes and Jesus replied, "Then give up your plans for your life for My plans for your life."

A few moments later, Jesus asked for the third time, "Peter, are you sure? Do you really love Me more than anything else in life?"

Hurt that He asked again, Peter said, "Jesus, You know everything. You know my heart and You can read my mind. You know I love You more than anything else."

Then Jesus said, "Then live your life according to My purpose for you."

As much as Peter wanted to reconcile with Jesus, Jesus wanted to reconcile with Peter even more. In this conversation Jesus forgave Peter, and placed Peter back into the same position with Him and the other disciples before the betrayal took place. Now He and Peter were completely reconciled!

In order to be truly free to be all God wants you to be, not only must you receive God's forgiveness, you must also do your part in forgiving others, seeking reconciliation to the best of your ability. Simply put, you and I are commanded to forgive others in the same way Jesus has forgiven us (Ephesians 4:32).

## 3. RECEIVE THE HOLY SPIRIT.

The first thing Jesus did the first time He met with His disciples after His resurrection was give them the Holy Spirit (John 20:22). Then, just before His ascension, He tells them to return to Jerusalem and wait for the Holy Spirit.

Why should they wait to receive something they have already received?

From the time Jesus walked out of the tomb until this present day, every person who believes in the resurrected Jesus receives the Holy Spirit. But there is a difference in Holy Spirit presence and Holy Spirit power. It's a difference, not in *quantity*—the moment you believed you received all the Spirit there is to receive, but in *quality*—you have all the Spirit, but does the Spirit have all of you? You will not be all Jesus wants you to be until you allow His Spirit to have all of you.

## 4. WALK IN FAITH.

Do you remember the conversation between Nate and Tommy? Tommy said he would only believe Jesus was alive if he was able to see Him and touch His scars. And who can blame him? Isn't that how you would have been? Have you ever thought it would be easier to believe in Jesus if you had been an eyewitness to all He did?

Well, when Tommy (some people call him Doubting Thomas) finally saw Jesus and was able to touch Him, Jesus said to Thomas, "Because you have seen Me, you have believed; blessed are those who have not seen and yet have believed" (John 20:29). The bottom line is this: following Jesus is a walk of faith, and it is only through faith that you can be all you can be.

# 5. GO OUT AND CHANGE YOUR WORLD.

Each semester, I ask my Sociology classes the following question, "How many of you are the first person in your family to go to college?"

There are always a few in every class who raise their hands. Some of those who do also tell me they are the first person in their family to have graduated from high school. I know teachers should not play favorites, but I can't help but admire those in my classes who are doing something no one else in their family has ever done. I tell them, I hope they realize that what they are doing is going to change the direction of, not just their life, but their family for generations to come. I teach for students like that.

But I follow Jesus because I want to change the world, or at least my little part of the world. Whatever dreams you have for yourself, God has bigger dreams because He wants you to be a world changer, and He wants you to start in your neighborhood. Before His ascension He said to His disciples, "All authority in heaven and on earth has been given to me. Therefore go and make disciples of all nations, baptizing them in the name of the Father and of the Son and of the Holy Spirit, and teaching them to obey everything I have commanded you. And surely I am with you always, to the very end of the age" (Matthew 28:18-20). Then, right before His ascension, Jesus told His followers to go to Jerusalem and wait for the Holy Spirit. Once they received the Holy Spirit, they would receive power to be His witnesses, first in "Jerusalem, and in all Judea and Samaria, and to the ends of the earth." (Acts 1:8).[9] Change the world, but start at home.

Pastor Dave never wanted to be a pastor. To be honest, the thought never entered his mind. As a teenager he had two loves: rock-n-roll and girls. At best, he was a nominal Christian, but nothing too serious. After graduating from high school, Dave went to the state university. He wanted to play music, and he wanted to be a lawyer.

That was during the 1970s and his college campus, like many others in our nation, got caught up in the "Jesus

Peoplc" movement.[10] Dave and some of his friends placed their faith in the resurrected Christ. Soon, he was having Bible studies in his dorm room. Gradually the group grew and by the time they graduated from college, that group of 1970 hippies had formed a church with Dave serving as pastor. Thirty five years later, Pastor Dave is still the pastor of that church and they are still attracting wild-eyed college students with wild ideals. He and his church have a heart for their own city, reaching people who are far from God; and their influence travels across the world. Pastor Dave would be the first to tell you that before he committed his life to Christ, he had big plans for his life, but those plans would not have changed his world. Pastor Dave would tell you that the way to succeed, the way to fulfill your life's purpose and be the best you can possibly be, is by following Jesus with all you have and all you are.

Jesus was just as human as you and me. Yes, He was God, but He was also fully human. He had the same struggles, the same emotions, the same temptations, and the same ups and downs as you. From the world's perspective, He failed, but in reality He lived a full and complete life, accomplishing all God wanted Him to accomplish.

And now He says it's your turn!

He rose from the dead; He forgave you of your sins; He has given you His Spirit; He has empowered you to walk in faith. You have, within you, the potential to change your world.

What are you waiting for?

# ENDNOTES

[1] The following conversation between Nate and Tommy is conjecture, loosely based on accounts found in the gospels. Nate is short for Nathanael, and Tommy is short for Thomas, both disciples of Jesus.

[2] It was at this meeting, on a mountain in Galilee, that Jesus gave the Great Commission, saying, "All authority in heaven and on earth has been given to me. Therefore go and make disciples of all nations, baptizing them in the name of the Father and of the Son and of the Holy Spirit, and teaching them to obey everything I have commanded you. And surely I am with you always, to the very end of the age" (Matthew 28:18-20).

[3] The story of Cleo ("Cleopas") is found in Luke 24:13-35. Nothing is known of Cleopas except for what Luke says, and the Bible doesn't say his wife was with him. The usual title of this story is "The Emmaus Road."

[4] John 20:25.

[5] Luke 24:45-49.

[6] Luke 24:50-51, italics added. The Ascension is also recorded in Mark 16:19.

[7] The conversation is based on John 21:15-19.

[8] John 21:3.

[9] Acts 1:8.

[10] Starting in the mid 1960s, continuing through the 1970s, the Jesus People movement was a revival that spread through the hippie community in and outside of college campuses across the United States.

## Questions for Discussion

1. Jesus said in John 14:12 that His followers would do even greater things than He did. How is that possible? Does it seem that His followers have done greater things? Why or why not?

2. Five things were mentioned in this chapter that we can do to continue the ministry of Jesus in our world. What were those five things? Which one do you think is the most important? Why?

3. How can you apply each of the five things from question #2 into your life? How can you encourage others to do the same?

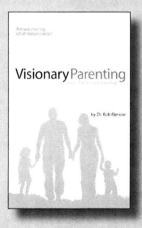

*Magazine Devotional? WOW!*

# Devotional Magazines for the entire Family!

*Michael would love this!*

## The best way to develop a strong youth group is to invest in the spiritual development of children.

*That's D6!*

D6 Devotional Magazines for the entire family equip, motivate, and resource parents to drive faith at home. Everyone studies the same Bible theme at the same time. This gives dads, moms, and grandparents a head start on having faith talks, conversations that matter, and teachable moments that will last a lifetime.

*Cool writers!*

Inside these trusted resources you will find not only daily scriptural devotions, but also regular columns and articles by **Dave Ramsey, Answers in Genesis, Jim Burns, Candice Watters, Sean McDowell, Mark Matlock, Brandon Heath, Fred Stoeker, John Trent, and many others.**

Our award winning D6 Kids magazines are packed with daily devotions, articles, games, puzzles, activities, and more!

Churches can order in bulk or families can subscribe online at D6family.com.

*helping parents reconnect to their kids!*

**Customizable for churches!**
For more information call
**800.877.7030**

CPSIA information can be obtained at www.ICGtesting.com
Printed in the USA
LVOW011928091111

254181LV00003B/6/P